The High School Survival Guide

Your Roadmap to:

- ☑ Studying
- ☑ Socializing
- ☑ Succeeding

D0958248

STUDY WITH JESS

Jessica Holsman

ISBN 978-1-63353-396-7

To my dear parents,
With all my love and gratitude

Table Of Contents

Introduction

Welcome

From the young age of fifteen, I knew I wanted to take on a profession that involved helping people. For many years, the thought of becoming a clinical psychologist sparked my interest. I never wanted to work in a desk job, spending the majority of my days in a high rise building, overlooking the city and its perfectly manicured gardens. Deep down, I knew that whatever I would end up doing, it needed to involve working with people, not for them. I guess that's why I was drawn to the idea of becoming a psychologist, because I wanted to be able to connect with others; to be the one to make them feel heard and guide them through pivotal stages in their lives.

Knowing that my performance in school was essential for helping me achieve my goal, I spent the majority of my final high school years hidden away in the school library. I was determined to pour all of my efforts into my studies and give myself the best chance of getting into one of the top universities in the state. Fueling my desire to succeed in school was my deep appreciation for my education, as I was raised to see it as a powerful tool that could be used to lead me down an avenue of endless possibilities. I just had to decide how I wanted to use it and which path to take. Growing up, my parents worked incredibly hard and made many sacrifices in order to give my sister and I an excellent education. Their efforts never went unnoticed and they certainly played a significant role in shaping my perception and the value I placed on my studies. Did I mention that my mother also happened to be a school teacher for over twenty-five years?

Giving a majority of my time to my studies was unfortunately at the expense of my well-being, as much of the valuable time I would usually spend tending to my own personal needs was cast aside. Perhaps it was due to the immense pressure that I put on myself in my final years of school, coupled with my competitive nature and perfectionist traits that I sported from a young age? Interestingly, my parents never seemed to place any pressure on me and would even excuse me from my responsibilities around the house. I no doubt placed more than enough pressure on myself for the three of us, which must explain why! My final years in high school were there to test me; although in hindsight, the level of difficulty found in the academic assessments were no match for the emotional obstacles that I would have to learn to navigate. My primary focus was my grades, and while proud of my academic achievements, I was left feeling tired and burnt out by the time I graduated from my final year of school.

It was only when I entered my first year at university and began studying my undergraduate degree in psychology at Monash University that my perception of my studies began to change. I shifted my mindset from being predominantly grade-focused to appreciating all of the opportunities that I had to expand my knowledge and grow as an individual. I began putting some much needed boundaries into place and structuring my study sessions differently, so that I wasn't left feeling restless or overwhelmed by the increasing workload that came with my degree. In fact, I remember being pushed academically and having more work than I did in high school, yet my memories of my time at university are only positive. Much of the changes that occurred around this time are thanks to the close friendships I made on campus. My friends and I acted as our own constant and unconditional support systems; encouraging each other when those major assignments and exams rolled around, studying together and sharing our methods and tricks. I soon learned that there were more ways to study than I had realized and that by incorporating different learning techniques that I actually enjoyed into my study sessions, the time that I spent studying became more effective, productive and yielded greater results. I stopped re-writing essays ten times in order to memorize them and instead, started reaching for bright colored markers and covering sheets of cardboard with illustrations that resembled key points, ideas and themes – even if they did look like meaningless or bizarre images to anyone else!

After completing my undergraduate degree, I decided to enroll in the postgraduate diploma of psychology course at Deakin University. Although only a one-year course, it felt as though I learned more in that one year than in any other throughout my education. I left with nothing but positive memories and my learning experience was enriched beyond my expectations. I graduated with honors and despite my ongoing efforts throughout the year, I couldn't help but feel surprised and thrilled with such an outcome! Between my friends, the lecturers, tutors and my supervisors, I couldn't have felt more supported either. There is no doubt in my mind that it was their collective effort to assist me, coupled with their evident passion for education that continued to ignite my love for learning.

Looking back at the age of twenty-five as a university graduate, I wish I could have told my younger self what I know now. It certainly would have saved me a lot of anxiety and stress in my final years of school! At times, I feel as though my perfectionist traits and undue pressure that I placed on myself robbed me of fully enjoying what is meant to be some of the most exciting years of our lives. This realization is none other than what drove me to start my YouTube channel Study With Jess shortly after I graduated. I never expected that my love for learning would take me down such an interesting and exciting pathway in life, and while it started as a way for me to creatively share my knowledge and put my study skills to good use, it became so much more in such a short time. I remember the first email I received from a viewer and reading about how my videos had helped get her through what she described as a challenging time in her life. That I was inspiring and motivating students to study, empowering them, and helping them look towards their future, that was all I needed to know. That I had truly found my life's purpose. Even though I don't believe that my future holds a career in psychology anymore, I know that the life lessons and skills I learned throughout school and university are what brought me to this point in my life. Who would have thought that I would go from being a "future psychologist" to "YouTuber, entrepreneur and now published author" in such a short time frame!

A lot has certainly changed since my high school days; my career choice, my skill set and my perception of my studies, however much of the same challenges, worries and concerns of students entering their final years of school still remain.

It's easy to fall into the trap of focusing solely on grades; forgetting why you are studying in the first place and what it is that you aim to get out of your time at school. Don't forget, your experience at school and your education are a privilege and your opportunity to not only expand your knowledge and skill-set, but also grow as an individual. Of course your grades are important, however getting good grades does not need to come at the expense of your own health and social life. You can excel in school academically and thrive as an individual as well!

Now ask yourself:

"Do I want to improve my grades?"
"Am I ready to enhance my study skills?"
"Am I ready to have an amazing time in high school?"

If you've answered 'yes' to any of the above questions then I strongly encourage you to keep reading! All of my secrets for enjoying high school and excelling academically can be found here in this book! I've made it my mission to help students around the world discover their love for learning, to feel motivated and inspired to get their work done and to maximize their full potential. Whilst I can't be physically present to answer all of your questions in person, this is my way of being there to support and guide you through this exciting new stage in your life. This is my high school survival guide. xo

Getting Ready For a New School Year

As a student, I always used to look forward to going back to school. Don't get me wrong, I definitely enjoyed my holidays and having the chance to catch up with all of my family and friends was always at the top of my list! In fact, those six weeks of holidays at the end of the school year never felt like they were long enough and for some reason, the final few weeks seemed to fly by. Despite my efforts, there was no way of making time slow down so that I could enjoy just one more sleepover, pool party or beach day with my closest friends.

There was one thing however, that always seemed to get me excited about going back to school. You guessed it - shopping for brand new school supplies! I remember walking down the stationery isles, pushing my trolley and being on high alert for new pens, notebooks and folders that were sporting the latest trends for the year. With every few meters that my trolley and I would cover, I would excitedly point and gesture to my mother to come and see what I had found. Notebooks were not pieces of lined pages bound together - at least, to me they weren't. They were blank canvases, ready to be colored with my knowledge. Highlighters - my paintbrushes, transforming my notes into pieces of art and pens and pencils - tools for transcribing my thoughts and organizing all of the questions that came with each new lesson throughout the year. Once home from my shopping adventure, I would tip open my bags, spread everything across the living room floor and inspect my newly made purchases. Then, I would spend the following few days deliberating which designs, photos and wrapping paper I should use to cover all of my binders and exercise books, before attempting the challenge of laminating them. Much to my parents' dismay, the living room floor would temporarily be transformed into my and my older sister's art space, as we cut, glued and colored in preparation for the new school year.

While a lot has changed since my days of school supplies shopping, my love for stationery has remained. I love how a new folder or a set of pencils can help someone look forward to a new school year, give them the motivation to pay just that little bit more attention in class, and take pride in getting their work done!

The Essentials

When it comes to getting ready for a new school year, having the right textbooks and stationery for class should be first on your list of to-do's. Make sure to access your book list well in advance to ensure you have all of your necessary books in time for class. As for the rest of your supplies, consider making a checklist so that you can go into stores with a plan of attack and feel confident that you have remembered to purchase all of your must-have items for the new school year. Speaking from experience, it can also be easy for that small list of items in your head to gradually expand as you stroll down the stationery and work organization isles. In just a few minutes, your trolley goes from being comfortably full, to looking more and more like a clearance bin, with every kind of pen, pencil, eraser and folder somehow being justified as a necessity for having a successful school year! One piece of advice when trying not to overfill your trolley with excessive items is to first go through your existing supplies and make a note of anything that is still in good condition and that you could take through with you into the new school year. Perhaps your folders are still in good condition or your packet of highlighters has a few hundred pages of color-coding left in them? Even if there are only a few items that don't need replacing, not having to buy more of these will save you money!

3 Money Saving Tips!

If you are trying to stick to a budget then here are three easy ways to save:

1. DIY your school supplies and transform old stationery and binders into personalized pieces that look brand new! Pay a visit to your local arts and craft store and pick up some supplies such as colored sheets of paper, paint and washi tape. Like I always say, "why buy it when you can DIY it?"

2. Buy your textbooks second hand. See whether someone in the year above you is looking to sell his or her textbooks from the previous year or even consider purchasing second hand books off a website.

3. Speak to someone in the year above you and find out if it is unlikely that you will be using any of your textbooks for extended periods of time. If you aren't going to need the textbook for very long, borrow it from the school library and photocopy the necessary chapters.

~ Use my back-to-school supplies shopping list as a guide for buying all of the necessary items you will need to stay organized throughout the new school year. Tick off any items you already have from the previous year, before heading to your office supply store and beginning to work your way down the list! ~

The Great Debate: Binders Vs. Folders

The need for new school supplies always seems to spark interest in the ongoing debate of whether it is best to use binders or folders in high school when trying to stay organized. On top of this, there is the question of whether having a separate binder or folder for each subject is preferable to having one that can be used for all subjects.

To answer the first question, it's important to highlight both the benefits and the limitations of binders and folders. While each makes for excellent storage and organization solutions for all of your class notes and handouts, they do differ significantly in a couple of areas. Unlike folders, using binders will also give you the option of writing your notes on loose sheets of paper. If you happen to take a lot of detailed notes in class, then you can add more sheets of paper to your binder as you go, rather than needing to purchase a second notebook later in the year. This does mean that you will need to take your binder home each night to complete your homework – something some students perceive as an inconvenience. In addition to the flexibility of adding pages to your binder, you also have the option of clipping and carrying accessories inside, such as

My Back-To-School Shopping List

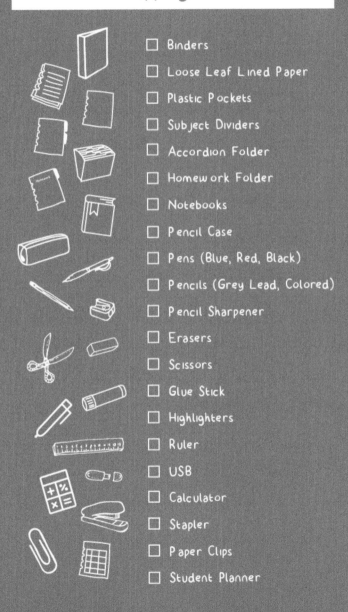

- [ ] Binders
- [ ] Loose Leaf Lined Paper
- [ ] Plastic Pockets
- [ ] Subject Dividers
- [ ] Accordion Folder
- [ ] Homework Folder
- [ ] Notebooks
- [ ] Pencil Case
- [ ] Pens (Blue, Red, Black)
- [ ] Pencils (Grey Lead, Colored)
- [ ] Pencil Sharpener
- [ ] Erasers
- [ ] Scissors
- [ ] Glue Stick
- [ ] Highlighters
- [ ] Ruler
- [ ] USB
- [ ] Calculator
- [ ] Stapler
- [ ] Paper Clips
- [ ] Student Planner

ring bound compatible pencil cases and rulers. If you are one to often forget to bring your pencil case and important stationery to class then this is a big plus! While binders do make for convenient storage solutions for carrying all of your notes and stationery essentials, their ability to hold all of your handouts is limited. In contrast, using a folder can often provide you with greater storage space for handouts and articles. Accordion or expandable folders are best because you can categorize your work according to the subtopics you are learning in class.

As for determining whether to keep a separate folder or binder for each subject, ultimately, the choice is yours. If you tend to get lots of handouts that need to be filed for each subject or repeatedly find yourself adding to your set of detailed notes, then it might be worthwhile to keep a separate folder or binder for each of your subjects. This way, all of your notes and handouts will be carefully organized and you can avoid having to resort to cramming all of your many papers inside!

Out With The Old And In With The New

Apart from needing to decide on how you plan to organize your work throughout the year, it's also important to spend some time organizing last year's notes. As you enter high school, the workload is known to become increasingly complex and the amount of notes and handouts you receive will likely grow as well. With each year that you progress forward along your academic journey, you will no doubt notice your teachers building on the material and skills that you learned during the previous year. For this reason, I highly recommend holding onto your old class notes. While some students do, others admit to throwing out their old class notes or even confessing to tearing out pages as a means for stress relief following their end of year exams. I was not one of them. In fact, ever since my kindergarten teacher sent me home with my first finger painting, my mother has made it her mission to create what looks a lot like a shrine to commemorate all of my work from school!

While it's certainly not necessary to keep notes from as long ago as your primary school years, it can serve you well in the future to organize and hold onto the notes you take in high school. Keep your notes for at least one to two years incase you need to refer back to them in the future. Set aside as little as one afternoon during the holidays to sought through your old class notes and file them somewhere safe. If you have typed your notes, it can be useful to have them bound and neatly organized into one book that you can easily flip through. Folders make for convenient storage solutions for all of your loose handouts, while you might like to keep your old notebooks organized in a set of magazine racks or line them up next to each other in your closet.

Getting A Head Start

Another important part of preparing for a new school year involves familiarizing yourself with your class texts. Use your spare time wisely during the holidays and consider opting for one of your class texts as your book of choice for the month. Make it an enjoyable exercise by setting aside some time each week to sit on the couch curled up with a cup of tea, or for those of you who are fortunate enough to spend your holidays somewhere warmer, by the pool or lying on the beach. Reading your texts in advance will give you a competitive edge, freeing up your time during the semester and allowing you to focus less on the specific outcomes in the book and more on analyzing the characters and key underlying themes throughout the story!

My Top 5 Tips
For Going Back To School

 Purchase your school supplies and textbooks during the holidays.

 Buy your textbooks second hand to save money.

 Organize and store your old class notes somewhere safe incase you need to refer back to them.

 Use binders or folders to organize your class notes and handouts.

 Familiarize yourself with your class texts before starting back at school.

I've always had a love for performing; getting up on stage, singing, dancing and acting in front of crowds of people. It's no wonder I spent most of my teenage years pursuing a career in dance. Somehow, I continually managed to schedule my jazz, ballet and tap classes around my increasingly demanding school calendar. Looking back, some of my most treasured memories from school involved performing. In fact, one of my mother's favorite stories to tell at the dinner table involves my first ever performance at my school soirée. I was six years old at the time and my class was asked to put on a short dance. Being my stubborn self and also unable to control the music and rhythm that was coursing through my little body, I decided to scrap the choreography my teacher had taught us and showcase my own dance moves halfway through the performance. There I was, bopping and grooving to the music, heading towards stage left and moving further and further away from my classmates! Lucky for me, the event has been documented in a series of photos, so that I will never forget it.

From my debut solo-esqué performance in first grade, to later choreographing the dances for my middle school play, being involved in different events was something that played a significant role in shaping my school experience. Every semester, the excitement and feelings of anticipation would resurface with each new application that was pinned on the school notice board. Sometimes, I was eager to make a specific role, however no role was too small to me. In fact, one year I was assigned the role of a lobster in a dance number that my drama teacher somehow viewed as an artistic take on the ten plagues in the story of Moses and the Pharaoh... Whatever the opportunity, my friends and I always jumped at the chance to be part of the school plays and one year, we even collaborated to write the script!

I didn't just see these events as a chance to showcase my talents. They were opportunities to spend time with my closest friends and even form bonds with other students; students that I wouldn't have normally socialized with during my lunch breaks when my friends and I would sit on the benches and catch up on the latest news and dare I say, gossip. Sometimes, when rehearsals ran late into the evenings, we would all walk down the street and grab a bite to eat for dinner. Suddenly, age and gender didn't matter anymore. That girl in the year below me whom I failed to take notice of, suddenly became one of my closest friends, while that boy in the year above me who I thought couldn't possibly have known who I was, began showing a genuine interest and striking up conversations. I liked how sharing a common interest could always break down social barriers and lead to lasting friendships.

The Benefits Of School Spirit

The start of a new school year brings with it new and exciting opportunities! While it's easy to forget when you're staring at a pile of textbooks that are stacked up on your desk or feeling their full weight as you pick up your school bag, there is more to school than homework, studying and grades. School is meant to be fun! Your teacher's want you to enjoy your final years of school and take with you positive memories that you will look back on and cherish. Sounds crazy right? Perhaps it is because there is such an enormous focus on getting good grades in order to get into a desirable college, that from time to time, extra-curricular activities and opportunities to show school spirit unfortunately get overlooked. Your time at school is limited, so make sure to take full advantage of everything your school has to offer. There are many opportunities to get involved and show school spirit, from performing in school plays, joining clubs and attending matches or games, to forming committees, entering competitions and hosting charity drives and school fêtes. Getting involved in a range of activities will benefit you in many ways and help to shape your experience at school. Ultimately, it's up to you to take personal responsibility for how you plan on spending your final years at school. The choices you make regarding how you spend this time are a reflection of your overall perception of school and have the potential to influence your attitude towards your studies.

 Work-life Balance

Apart from taking pride in your school, taking advantage of all the opportunities that it has to offer outside of the classroom can also help you achieve a healthy work-life balance. Take it from someone who once had fallen victim to retreating into a little study cave for months on end only to reappear when that final assessment or exam was over! Re-directing your attention towards something other than your homework and exam calendar will remind you that there is more to school than what you learn in class. Allowing yourself to take even a little time out to do something besides studying will also help to keep you from getting burnt out during the year. You are allowed to give yourself a break from the books. In fact, you'll likely notice yourself feeling more refreshed and ready to tackle your homework when you do!

 Forming Friendships

The friendships and bonds you develop during school also play a significant role in shaping your experience. Making friends at school can however be more of a challenge for some than others. Whether you are new to the school, a little shy or things have gone south in your existing friendship circle, getting involved in a range of school activities is an excellent way to meet other students who share a common interest of yours. After all, it is a lot easier to start up a conversation with someone you know you already have something in common with! Personally, I felt grateful to have found a group of people who not only accepted but also encouraged me to pursue whatever I felt passionate towards. It certainly helped me to come out of my shell and feel more confident. I strongly believe that acceptance, coupled with encouragement, has the potential to be incredibly empowering.

 Preparing For The Future

Whilst getting involved in school activities can help to create a positive learning environment and enrich your time at school overall, it also has the ability to prepare you for the real world. It provides you with an array of opportunities to explore and develop various skills, talents and traits that will serve you well in the future, regardless of your career choice. Even if you are unsure of exactly what it is that you want to do when you finish school, exposing yourself to numerous opportunities to get involved will no doubt come in handy. Rather than choosing to only take part in activities that you feel will directly assist you in progressing further down a particular career path, open yourself up to the possibility of taking part in something that genuinely sparks your interest. All skills you learn in school and throughout life for that matter are transferable. I may not have pursued a career in dance, but being a dancer and choreographer in my school plays taught me a lot about leadership and teamwork, two skills that are necessary and highly regarded in the workforce!

Igniting Your School Spirit

Perhaps you are eager to get involved but find yourself unsure of where to start, or maybe this is the first time that you have thought about taking part in a school activity or initiative? Now that I've covered a range of benefits associated with showing school spirit, it's only fair that I also share my tips for getting involved! I recommend that you start by finding out what sort of opportunities your school provides for students to get involved and consider whether any of them interest you. Your teachers are often a great place to start because they will likely have a good idea of what is being offered. Then, to help you filter through the list of opportunities, consider not only the things that you enjoy, such as your hobbies, and the skills you possess, but also causes that you feel passionate towards. Choosing something that you feel strongly towards, means that you will feel personally invested and will be more likely to remain committed to it throughout the year.

While every school is different and may not offer the same opportunities for their students, it is always an option to think about starting up a new group or club and recruiting members. Starting something new shows initiative and also provides other students with an opportunity to get involved. When I was in high school, my best friend and I decided to raise money for a charity. After an intense class discussion about the fact that many children in developing countries are deprived of access to education, we decided to raise money to support an organization that helps to send many of these children to school. We ended up selling blue ribbons to our peers and teachers that were to be worn on their collars for the week, in an attempt to show their support for a cause we felt strongly towards. What started as two of us cutting and pinning ribbons in my bedroom, became something that more and more of my friends decided to get involved in.

If you don't find yourself being internally pulled towards any particular cause, yet you are still looking for something to get involved in at school, then the school play is an excellent option! I used to think that to be part of the school play meant that you had to enjoy performing, however not everyone enjoys getting up on stage and shining under the spotlight in front of large numbers of people. The school play offers every kind of role, each with varying levels of commitment. Importantly, they don't all require you to foster a love for performing. If you don't mind getting your hands dirty and want to exercise your creativity, then helping out with designing the set is always a fun option! If you happen to be tech savvy, another important role is being in charge of the lighting and music. Speaking of music, did I mention that the school band plays an important role and is another way to get involved? I may not have been known for my musical talents at school, considering I did only learn how to play the piano up until the age of eleven, however for those of you who spend a significant portion of your time afterschool rehearsing your musical instrument, the school band is an excellent way to showcase your musical talents! Whatever role you choose, the school play is a microcosm for showcasing skills in creativity, writing, performing, technology and more!

Of course, watching and cheering for your peers on opening night is also a form of school spirit. Never underestimate the importance of showing up to support your school in all its events. Attending charity drives, your school fête or important matches and games are all ways of getting involved in all that your school has to offer. Just because you are not hosting, does not mean you are not helping! Being present and taking the time out of your busy study schedule to attend important events at school will leave you with lasting memories and help to create a sense of belonging.

My Top 5 Tips
For Unleashing Your School Spirit

 Be willing to take time out from studying to get involved in school activities and initiatives.

 Whatever the activity or cause, make sure you are passionate about it.

 If you feel strongly about a cause, consider starting up your own club or committee.

 Get involved in your school play and use it as an opportunity to showcase existing talents or learn new skills.

 Remember, school spirit can be as simple as showing up to support your peers in an event!

Socializing In 👍 School

Every day, as the lunch bell would sound, my friends and I would pack up our books, grab our food from our lockers and head to the school yard where we would all meet. Every friendship group would have their own usual meeting spot and to the fifteen of us, ours was prime real estate. We would all sit in a circle, eating our lunch and catch each other up on the latest stories and events that happened during class that morning. Despite the occasional disagreement between a few of us – something that was bound to happen when you're talking about fifteen teenage girls – we all got along and I was lucky to have such great friends throughout school.

It was only when I started my second-last year of school that all of a sudden I felt as though I lost interest in the daily chit chat at lunch and started to retreat into my shell. I became more quiet than usual and didn't feel as though I had much to contribute to the conversations that everyone was having... It all began shortly after a few of the girls in my friendship circle moved to another school, resulting in a change in the dynamics of the group. A lot of my friends started hanging out with other students in my year at lunch and shifted friendship circles. I was still close with a lot of them, but I didn't know their new friends and so I didn't follow to sit with them at lunch. At first, I felt upset and resisted the social changes that were happening around me. I missed having a tight-knit friendship group. Although I could have continued to allow myself to stay focused on the fact that I didn't feel as though I belonged to any one particular group, I decided instead on changing my outlook. I became grateful for all of the close friends I did have - even if I didn't happen to share the same social circle with many of them anymore. I used my situation as an opportunity to get to know the other students in my year that they were friends with and alternated between sitting with one group of people one day, and another the next. Not feeling as though I "belonged" to a particular group was actually quite liberating because I felt as though I could hang out with whomever I wanted on any given day. I ended up befriending a lot of the people that my friends would sit with and over time, some became close friends of mine whom I still keep in touch with today.

By the time I started my final year at school, many of the social barriers that I perceived had come down. No one really had a "group" anymore and everyone was friendly with one another. In fact, we would spend much of our time with the people who were studying the same subjects as us, as the common goal of succeeding in our final year brought many of us closer together.

Building A Support System

Making friends and socializing is an important part of your high school experience. Your friends are probably going to be the ones who can relate most to what you are going through and will be there to support and encourage you along the way. Not only are you each other's emotional support systems; bringing light to challenging or stressful situations, you are also there to help each other reach your academic goals. I most certainly would not have done as well as I did in school and university if it wasn't for the help of my friends and the hours we spent in the library reviewing and teaching each other the material for our final exams! One thing when making friends at school that I would advise is not to get caught up in numbers.

Remember, quality over quantity! It's always better to have a handful of close friends who you feel comfortable around and can trust in, as opposed to surrounding yourself with people who leave you feeling uncomfortable, fail to include you, or make you feel bad about yourself. True friends should build you up. They should not tear you down!

Making Friends

Whether you've moved to a new school or want to get to know the rest of the students in your grade, making new friends can sometimes be daunting. Even though getting outside of your comfort zone can make you feel uneasy, – that is why it's called your comfort zone after all – it's important that you put yourself out there and make an effort. What's the worst thing that can happen? You approach someone and they don't reciprocate? If someone isn't going to be nice back to you, then chances are you don't want to be friends with him or her anyway!

If you're trying to expand your social horizons then make sure you are putting yourself out there and creating new opportunities for you to meet others. As I already mentioned earlier, getting involved in a range of activities, events or clubs that your school offers is an excellent way to make new friends as you explore your common interests together. If you're also looking to get to know your classmates better, then try sitting next to different students each day. You're not going to make new friends by sitting next to your 'bestie' time and time again! Changing up your seating arrangements in class will also give you the chance to partner with new students in group assignments and projects. Teachers often allocate students to groups based on who they are seated next to, so use this as an opportunity to get to know your peers.

Now, when it comes to breaking the ice and striking up a conversation, a good way to start is by giving someone a compliment. I don't mean that you should throw around empty compliments, such as telling everyone that you like their hair, clothes or jewelry. Instead, try and think of something personal that you truly value about them. If you are genuinely impressed by a piece of art they made in class, an interesting point they raised in a group discussion, or the way you saw them treat someone, make sure to let them know. I honestly believe that we don't compliment or give each other recognition enough, so I always try to see the good in others and let them know!

Once you've started talking to them, take it as an opportunity to get to know more about them. Ask them questions about themselves and show that you are genuinely interested in what they have to say. Try finding out what they thought of the topic you are learning in class, what they did on the weekend or what they are doing after school. What person doesn't like being given the chance to talk about themselves?

As useful as these tips may be, when it comes to making real and lasting friendships, the best piece of advice I can give you is to be yourself. There's no point trying to impress people by pretending you share the exact same interests if you don't. Besides, pretending to be someone you're not will get tiring after a while and you'll soon realize that your friendship is only skin deep. Real friends will accept you for who you are, quirky traits and all!

Fitting In

I hate to be the bearer of bad news, but things may not always go smoothly. It's all part of life and sometimes you and your friends won't see eye to eye. Other times, you might experience challenges with other students in your school that can leave you feeling uncomfortable, upset or even doubting in yourself. It's important to remember your support systems and surround yourself with people who have your best interests at heart. Never feel embarrassed or be too proud to reach out for help and speak up. Most importantly, always know that you are never alone.

 Dealing With Peer Pressure

Everyone wants to feel as though they belong and are accepted. No one likes to be kept out of the loop or made to feel like an outcast. Unfortunately, trying to fit in can sometimes mean feeling as though you need to act a certain way or do something you wouldn't normally do. Whether it's feeling like you need to be in a relationship, drink alcohol at parties, dress differently, or be mean to someone else, just because your friends are doing it, doesn't mean you should, too. Of course, it's okay to want to fit in, however when it means compromising your morals and values, I strongly advise that you think twice! Remember, it's okay to be that black sheep and not follow the rest of the herd.

Dealing with peer pressure can be tricky. On one hand, you want to fit in and feel accepted by your peers, whilst on the other hand, you don't want to be someone you're not in order for them to like you. In any case, you should think about what is most important to you and how you want and deserve to be treated. If you feel as though someone is pressuring you to do something, consider confronting this person and letting him or her know how you feel. If you feel comfortable and think they will receive what you have to say without judgment, then it might be a helpful strategy to tackle the situation head on. Whatever the issue, it's always best to also talk to someone who you feel you can trust. Letting a parent, close friend, family member or even teacher know what is going on can help you feel supported and remind you that you are not alone. Often, they will also be able to help with some useful strategies to manage the situation. No matter what, it's important that you stay true to yourself and don't let what others do influence your judgment about what is right for you.

 Standing Up To Bullies

Another common issue you might encounter during school is bullying. Bullying takes a range of forms and can be online or offline, include name-calling, spreading false gossip and physical arguments. No matter what form it takes, it's never okay and you should never feel as though you deserve it or should have to tolerate it. There's really no one reason why some students become the target of bullying over others. I was certainly no exception and neither were several of my friends during school. Luckily for me, it wasn't something that escalated out of control or went on for very long.

When it comes to dealing with being bullied, there are always a few things that you should do. It can be difficult, but where possible, try and avoid engaging with the person who is bullying you. If someone is bullying you to your face, walk away. If it's online, block it and report it. Whatever you do, avoid fueling the fire and engaging with the other person. When you try not to show the other person that their behaviour is having a negative effect on you, the power they thought they had begins to diminish and the less likely they are to continue bothering you.

Something else to remember is that no matter what someone says, it's not personal. Sometimes being unique can make you a target for being bullied, however it doesn't mean you need to change who you are, what you like or what you do. You are perfect exactly how you are! Besides, do you know how many talented and famous artists, musicians and singers wouldn't be working today if they listened to those who tried to tear them down when they were younger? Whatever you love doing, do it! Giving up something that you are passionate about could leave you feeling more upset as you will be sacrificing a significant part of who you are, in the hopes that someone will finally accept you. Like I said, people make fun of others for a number of reasons. Whether it's out of jealousy, a dislike for people who are different to them or maybe they are having a challenging time with something in their own lives, remember, it's not personal. You don't need to start questioning yourself, going through an in-depth self-evaluation, critiquing yourself and trying to fit into their mold of what it means to be acceptable.

My last piece of advice if you find yourself being bullied is to always let either a parent or teacher know! There's no need to bottle up your feelings inside and keep it a secret. Again, confiding in an adult will help you to decide on how to best deal with the situation and make sure that you feel well supported. You have the right to feel safe at school and shouldn't have to go through a challenging situation alone.

My Top 5 Tips
For Socializing In School

 Get involved in school activities, clubs and committees to meet students whom you share a common interest with.

 Try giving someone a compliment as a way to break the ice and spark up a conversation.

 Get to know other students by asking them questions about themselves.

 Be yourself. True friends will accept you for who you are!

 Always talk to a parent or teacher and seek advice if you experience problems with friends or peers at school.

The Ideal Study Environment

When I was thirteen, my parents decided to renovate our house and build a second story. My sister and I had long outgrown our cozy three-bedroom one bathroom house – emphasis on the one bathroom please – and our parents were reminded of this all too frequently. We used to come home each afternoon from school, set ourselves up at the kitchen table and lay out our books and worksheets for that night. I always preferred working at the table, despite having a desk of my own. Perhaps it was a case of prioritizing, because I had chosen to use my desk as a place to store and display my growing collection of soft toys and photo frames. My father always believed that it was important to separate where we worked from where we slept, so he designed both our bedrooms upstairs to have an adjoining study. In the end, I think I was more excited about the fact that my room would finally be able to fit a double bed, however I soon realized just how valuable it was to have my own space to work in and think quietly, away from other distractions.

The majority of the time that I spent studying was probably at my desk, however as I entered my final years of high school I chose to study in libraries. I liked the idea that I could completely separate my studies from my home. I was able to leave my work and all of the mental chatter that came with it at the door. I saw my home as my own personal retreat, a place where I was able to finally unwind after a busy day filled with statistics equations, psychology theories and biology definitions. As my final exams drew nearer, my friends and I would venture into the city and study in the state library on the weekends. I remember the first time I went to study there. There were high ceilings covered in decorative plaster, old varnished parquetry floors, and grand study halls that housed hundreds of charming desks. It's enchanting interior certainly contrasted with the vibrant scene of hip hop and break dancers that would come to battle outside the entrance steps! When our focus would begin to wane, my friends and I would take a tea or hot chocolate break and cross the road to our favorite coffee shop. There, we would sit on the sofas upstairs and have group discussions about the books we were studying, brainstorming potential text response answers and formulating our arguments. Okay, so perhaps it wasn't as much of a study break as it was a good change of scenery? It was actually very helpful to change up the environment and the coffee shop was perfect for when we didn't need to be engaging in silent study. Also, being the tea lover that I am, I found those breaks to be very relaxing and a great way to recharge my batteries!

Deciding Where To Study

Whether you have your own separate study or tend to work in your bedroom, your local library, or a coffee shop, it's important to make sure that your environment is helping and not hindering your ability to study. Having a good study environment can increase your motivation and help maximize your productivity. A good study environment is however a highly individualized matter. That is, what's right for you may not be right for someone else! Just because your best friend prefers to study in his or her bedroom does not mean that your bedroom is the best place for you to get your work done, too. In fact, many of my friends used to study at home, while only a handful of my friends and I chose to study in the school library, where we felt we would be most productive.
If you're having trouble deciding where the best place for you to study is, then here are some questions to ask yourself:

"Am I easily distracted?"
"Do I tend to move around a lot if I am in my room?"
"Do people often interrupt my study sessions?"
"Do I prefer to discuss the information with others?"

If you found yourself answering "yes" to even one of these, it would be wise to strongly consider studying outside of your bedroom and opting for somewhere where you will less likely be distracted but also be able to discuss the material with others when need be. Studying in a library is usually your best bet, since there are areas to engage in group discussions, as well as silent study zones for when you want to avoid the chatter.

A Productive Study Space

While there are some students who seem to be able to study just about anywhere, I most certainly was not one of them! I remember seeing students sitting on the floor in the school corridor with an open textbook resting on their lap, while others would sometimes research essay topics in the school cafeteria and review class notes on the bus ride home. Each time I would be left wondering to myself how anyone could get past the first sentence on a page without getting distracted! If you're anything like me, then you will also likely benefit from having a designated study space where you can be your most productive self.

So what exactly are the key requirements that make for a productive study space? Personally, the following four tips have proven fundamental when I was trying to create my ideal study environment; a place where I felt comfortable, was motivated to study, and that enhanced my level of efficiency so that I could produce my best quality work!

◈ Limit Distractions

Before I get started on this first tip, I'd better check my social media and reply to that text message that just went off in the background! Just a minute...

Sound familiar? Too often we find ourselves chained to our phones and connected to social media. We know we shouldn't do it, but that sound of a new notification emits a wave of anxiety that feels like it will boil over if we don't check and respond to whomever or whatever is requiring our attention! I've certainly done this and still catch myself out every now and then. In reality, we happen to cause many of the distractions that we experience when trying to study and get our work done. On the upside, this means that they can be prevented but it's up to us. Temporarily detaching yourself from social media and the outside world can seem daunting, especially when people start suggesting website blockers and advising you to switch off your mobile phone until you've finished your work. If you happen to view these options as too extreme then consider at least turning your phone on silent or switching off your notifications while you study. I keep my phone on silent and somewhere away from my desk where I am less likely to glance over and feel the need to start scrolling through social media or responding to emails. I also tend to close my website browsers unless I am using them to research a topic, otherwise I find myself impulsively opening a new tab and procrastinating by watching entertaining clips on YouTube!

Some distractions are harder to control. If you study at home then you might have already had to deal with the interruptions of your family members. Even though their intentions are usually good, the persistent knocking on your

GETTING MY NERD ON

I'M CURRENTLY SOLVING THE MYSTERY OF PLANET EARTH PLEASE COME BACK LATER.

GENIUS IN PROGRESS

DO NOT DISTURB

door and ongoing interruptions can result in you losing your train of thought. Their updates and questions (that really can wait) are then received with frustration and result in a less than welcoming response that is usually followed by the slam of a door! One way to prevent these situations from happening in the future is to remind your family that you are studying and are not to be disturbed. One of the most thoughtful things that my mother made me when I was in my final years of studying was a do not disturb sign. I know, it really doesn't take much to impress me! I had repeatedly asked my parents and sister not to disturb me when I was studying, yet they consistently would forget and my study sessions would be interrupted with updates about when dinner would be ready, when my favorite show was starting and amusing things that my pets were doing outside. I know they meant well and so I did try not to let my frustrations out on them, but having a sign on my door made a huge difference. My mother ended up recycling one of my bag tags and hanging it on my door with quirky announcements - my favorite one being: "Genius in progress. Do not disturb!"

~ Cut out the do not disturb signs on the previous page and use them as a way to avoid interruptions and let your family know you are busy studying. Stick them on your door or cut them to size and place them inside a bag tag to hang on your door handle. ~

 ## Keep a Tidy Workspace

I've always prioritized setting aside some time each week to sought through any of my papers that are lying around on my desk and throw out any rubbish that is taking up valuable working space. Keeping a tidy workspace can help to enhance your productivity and stay organized, so it's important that everything on your desk has a place and anything that doesn't need to be there is put away! When I was studying, I would tend to spread my work out so that I could see everything, which is why I would try to keep on my desk only the necessary items that I needed at the time to complete my homework. Usually, my staple items would include my textbooks and handouts for a particular subject, my laptop, a pencil case and my planner. Any other supplies that I might need later would be stored away in boxes on my shelf or in my desk drawer, so that they would not clutter my workspace. Remember, when you create space in your study, you create space in your mind to think clearly!

 ## Create a Positive Environment

You might have heard that stress can be good for you; that it is known to even enhance your productivity and make you feel more alert. This is true, however only up to a certain point. When it comes to studying on a daily basis, you'll do your best work when you feel calm and relaxed. Your final years of school can be demanding and you'll likely spend more time studying than you previously have, so it's important that your study environment assists you in staying calm and feeling motivated. Consider your workspace to be your own personal sanctuary - your place of inspiration where your ideas begin to flow. Creating

5 Quick Tips For Keeping a Tidy Workspace!

1 Allocate a folder or use a set of stacking draws to file and separate your incoming handouts from your outgoing and already completed ones.

2 Label and store old assignments, tests and important handouts in a safe place in case you need to refer to them later in the year.

3 Scan important documents to reduce paper clutter and help you stay organized.

4 Set aside 10-20 minutes at the end of each week to clean out the clutter on your desk.

5 If you have trouble deciding what to get rid of when cleaning your workspace, use the handy motto, "when in doubt, throw it out!"

a calming atmosphere can be as simple as burning an essential oil such as lavender, keeping an indoor plant or fresh flowers on your desk, or playing some instrumental classical music. I also like the idea of personalizing your workspace by displaying motivational quotes and images to get you into a more positive mindset and feeling determined to study. Even if you prefer to study outside of home, you can still apply the majority of these suggestions and transform any workspace into an inviting area for you to study.

 Get Comfortable

The last thing you want to have pulling your focus away from your work is the feeling of being uncomfortable! Whether your chair is too low, your computer screen - too close, your lamp - too dim, or the room - too hot, these are all things that can impact your ability to work efficiently. In order to make sure you are studying in a comfortable environment, first thing's first; you need to set yourself up correctly. It might sound rigid or even unnecessary, however having the right posture is essential! Make sure your computer screen is at eye level and your feet are placed comfortably on the ground with your knees at ninety degrees. Trust me, it will save you from having to put up with sore shoulders, a stiff neck and back pain, after hours of studying day after day, week after week, and month after month! It was only after I kept getting neck pain that I finally realized that I needed to set myself up properly at my desk. Oh and by the way, yes, this does mean that you should not be studying in your bed. Sorry to disappoint all of you who were thinking that since your bed is probably the most comfortable place you know, it must mean that it is also an optimal place to study... Your bed should be for sleeping and never for studying; otherwise you run the risk of taking a sneaky nap half way through what could have otherwise been a productive study session!

My Top 5 Tips

For Creating The Ideal Study Environment

 If you find yourself getting distracted at home, try studying at your school or local library.

 Limit potential distractions by refraining from going on your phone or surfing the Internet while studying.

 Set aside some time each week to tidy your desk and clean out the clutter!

 Create a calming and positive environment by personalizing your study space with your favorite items.

 Always study away from your bed!

An
Organized
Life

My father once told me not too long ago, "If you want something done, you should give it to a busy person." Well, I am definitely one of those busy people! I am always juggling several tasks, yet somehow manage not to neglect any of my responsibilities. I have noticed that it is in fact the people who live a busy life that tend to be the most productive, efficient and well organized. Once again my father was right!

Thinking back to my time in school, I remember being very organized. In hindsight, I guess I had to be. Apart from attending school, I spent most of my time in a dance studio in the city. Every afternoon as the school bell rang to signal the end of the day, I would eagerly pack up my bag and head towards the school gates where my mother would be waiting for me. I'd grab a snack that I had left in my lunchbox and begin reading over my notes in the car as we made our way home in peak hour traffic. Once home, I would head to my study, pull out my school diary and see what homework I had for the night. I'd usually manage to fit in an hour and a half of studying after school before taking a break to have dinner, change into my dance clothes, pack my dance bag and head out the door to catch the tram into the city. Jazz, tap, ballet, contemporary, lyrical and hip-hop – every style of dance had a special place in my heart. Did I mention I also took the occasional crumping class? After taking my first hip hop class at the age of fifteen in a grungy and slightly in need of a face-lift studio not far from where I lived, I fell deeper in love with dance and knew it was something that I had to pursue. I was determined to make it work! I knew however that I had to make sure my grades wouldn't suffer and so it meant organizing my days in such a way that enabled me to live out my passion while still getting an education and not over-extending myself. I've always believed that if something is truly important to you, then you will make time for it, regardless of all of the responsibilities you already have.

Finding the time to get all of my work done and still keep up my average wasn't easy at first. I realized that the key was sticking to a clear schedule and using my spare time as wisely as possible. I spent my free lessons and sometimes lunch breaks in the school library working on assignments. My planner became my lifesaver, never leaving my side and always reminding me of tasks that had somehow escaped my mind in the midst of an increasingly busy semester. My skills in organization became evident to everyone at dance practice, with my hip hop teacher one morning catching me with my head buried in a textbook between classes. He must have thought I was either the most studious person he'd ever met or the biggest nerd... It didn't matter though. Those thirty minutes between my contemporary and hip-hop class were the difference between showing up on Monday morning having done my report for psychology, and having to bear my teacher's look of disappointment as she hands out an afterschool detention. I'll take a quick study session over that situation any day!

Of course there were days when I needed to get my priorities straight and focus on my studies. Occasionally I would opt out from going to a dance class in order to study for an upcoming test, finish working on a group project or focus on studying for my final exams. Overall, I was able to balance the two quite nicely. Now, as I think back to my final years of school, I know I have my love of dance to thank for many of the skills I now possess in living an organized life!

Plan Your Days

Being an organized student means knowing how to best manage your time. As you enter your final years of school, you will probably begin to notice the workload as well as your responsibilities start to increase. In order to balance schoolwork, family responsibilities and extracurricular activities in high school and even later in life, my first suggestion is to invest in a planner! Using a planner or school diary is an excellent way to improve your organizational skills and help you to better manage a busy schedule. My planner has definitely made a huge difference to my level of productivity. I am also far less likely to forget small tasks now, because unlike the human head, nothing can be forgotten once it has been written down!

The first thing I like to do when I get a new planner is write down any major events and key dates for each month. This includes semester breaks, school camps, exam periods and any important dates relating to extracurricular activities, such as dance concerts, recitals or final games. Unlike when I was at university and could access my course outline or unit guide ahead of time, I could not access the exact dates for my exams or assignments before a new school year. My teachers would only disclose this information as the semester progressed, so if this is the case for you as well, be sure to write these down as soon as you can. Speaking of writing things down as soon as possible, when it comes to using a planner on a daily basis, make sure you document any homework and reminders right away! Writing your homework down while you are still in class will save you from forgetting to complete a piece of work and having to cram at the last minute. Being the organized person that I am, and also a big fan of visual cues. I recommend writing your homework down in different colors depending on the subject or class they are for. This way, they will stand out in your diary and make planning your study sessions easier.

Block It Out

In addition to helping remind you of which chapter in your chemistry book you need to read or which questions you need to answer for your English class tomorrow, your planner is also there to help structure your study sessions and budget your time effectively. As the workload begins to increase, you might begin to wish that there were more time in a day to complete all of those handouts, projects and papers. Now I don't have a magic genie lamp that you can rub in the hopes of having your wish granted, however even if there was an extra hour or two built into each day, would it really make all the difference? Ok, well maybe it would, although usually it comes down to how you are actually using your time. Like I said earlier, if something is really important, you will make time for it!

One tip that helped me better make use of my time was to block out my study sessions and break them up based on each subject. Allocating yourself specific times to study is a great way to reduce procrastination, since the act of writing down your 'study appointments' will help to keep you on track and get your work done. Most importantly, it can help to make the large workload seem less overwhelming as you begin to see that there is still enough time for you to tend to your other responsibilities – provided you stick to your schedule that is! Try and spend a couple of minutes at the start of your study sessions deciding how you could best organize your time. You can do this by considering how much homework you have for each subject and estimating the total amount of time you think you will need in order to complete the relevant work. Use your planner or diary to then block out when you plan to study for each subject, while still factoring in your other responsibilities. This way, you can be sure that you won't neglect any subjects since you will be giving each one its own allocated study timeframe. For example, after school each day I would open up my diary and gaze over my homework for the evening. Then, I needed to decide how much time I was going to spend on each subject, shading in the respective hours in different colors; blue for history, green for biology, yellow for English and red to represent math. Importantly, I would make sure to plan my study sessions around my other responsibilities and needs as well, such as when I was going to eat dinner or be at dance practice, so that I not only organized my school life, but my life as a whole.

To-Do Or Not To-Do

Whether your teachers have simultaneously decided to assign you a week's worth of readings and worksheets that are all 'conveniently' due on the same day, or you feel as though there are dozens of other responsibilities that require your attention, there is one way to get through it! One of the easiest and most effective ways to be organized is to create to-do lists. The simple act of keeping a notepad on your desk to write yourself reminders can help you clearly see all of the tasks that require your attention and ensure you don't forget any. Apart from acting as a handy reminder system, the reason I am such a huge advocate for creating to-do lists is because of their ability to make the large workload appear more manageable, by bringing structure into a study session. It can be easy to feel overwhelmed when thinking about all of the tasks that need to get done, however the act of writing them down has a way of easing anxieties and enabling us to focus on one task at a time. My advice when using to-do lists is to be realistic about how much you think you will be able to get done during each study session so that you can achieve your goals and be proud of them!

My Top 5 Tips
For Staying Organized

 Keep a planner or school diary to write down your homework and important dates and events throughout the year.

 Write down your homework as soon as you get it in class.

 Block out when you plan to study for each subject in your planner.

 Plan your study sessions around your extracurricular activities and personal responsibilities.

 Create to-do lists to help you keep track of your work.

Structuring Your Study Sessions

When I was much younger, roughly between the ages of six and nine years old, I remember coming home each afternoon from a busy school day and following my mother into the kitchen. There, she would sit me up on the counter, make me a snack and begin to quiz me about my day as she started to prepare dinner for the family. "What did you do?" "Who did you play with?" "What did you learn?" and of course the most important question of the day, "What homework do you have tonight?" As she began chopping the vegetables, I would talk to her about the daily events; the activities I did in class, my achievements for the day, the friends I made, and any problems or concerns that were occupying my mind. Afterwards, I would take out my books from my school bag and begin reading to her. Somehow, she would always manage to keep one eye on the food and the other on me. She would listen attentively to every word I pronounced, helping me whenever she heard a longer than usual pause that was often accompanied by a puzzled expression on my face. Once I had finished my homework, she would prop me off the kitchen counter, praise me for doing a good job, sign my homework diary and excuse me to go and play with my toys in my bedroom.

Although only a regular occurrence during my early years of school, forming such a routine from an early age certainly influenced how I viewed my schoolwork. Now, looking back as a university graduate, I have my mother to thank for the effective study habits and strong work ethic that have lead to my achievements.

The Right Time To Study

An important part of having a good study schedule involves knowing when you are at your most productive and alert self. There's no use trying to read those several chapters from your textbook late at night if you know you need a good nine hours of sleep to function the next day. Likewise, that essay you need to complete for English class is probably going to take a lot longer during the day if you happen to be a night owl, doing you best work when everyone's gone to sleep and there are less distractions around to deter your focus.

While afterschool activities or other personal commitments can sometimes dictate when you will be able to complete your work, try and aim to tackle your homework, big projects and important assignments during your peak-energy periods. Although it can be easy to let your study schedule be influenced by when your peers, friends or siblings study, each and every one of us tends to study best at different times of the day. I found that I was most productive during the day, so I chose to study when I would get home from school. I would usually start working from four-thirty, break for dinner around six-thirty and then resume studying for another hour or so, depending on the amount of work I had to complete that night. Although I wish I didn't need at least eight and a half hours of sleep each night, I certainly did try a few times to study late at night like some of my friends. Unfortunately, I soon realized that by this point, my poorly timed study sessions became unproductive. If I needed to spend some extra time reviewing my notes and studying for a test, I would set my alarm an hour earlier than usual and use that time to sneak in some extra studying before school. I found it was much more effective than staying up late and didn't leave me feeling as tired throughout the day.

Setting Time Limits

An increasing amount of homework means an increasing amount of time spent studying. Spending long periods of time studying can leave you tired and restless. Even if you happen to get into a "study zone" with no problem and feel as though you could study for hours, it doesn't necessarily mean that you should. I used to do this in high school until I noticed that my patterns of pulling extended study sessions were contributing to my increasing fatigue. Fortunately, there is reason to believe that studying less during each study session can help your brain consolidate information into your long-term memory more effectively. That's right, studying longer does not necessarily guarantee you better grades! I don't mean that you should be studying less overall, however taking a short break to get up and stretch or have a drink of water can help to make your study sessions more productive. You'll likely be most productive during the first twenty-five to thirty minutes of hitting the books. After this point, our focus tends to plateau, before drastically falling. This means that if you are studying for hours on end, your time spent trying to tackle your homework is likely becoming unproductive. What's more, it can leave you feeling tired and restless, and finding it difficult to focus. No wonder after all of those hours trying to persevere, you finally realize you've read the same sentence multiple times!

Instead, try to structure your study sessions by organizing them into thirty-minute blocks. Studying for no more than thirty minutes at a time can help you maximize your productivity, stay focused and produce your highest quality work! Try and break up your study sessions with a short five to ten-minute break to re-charge your batteries and re-fuel your brain, so that you are able to absorb the information better.

Prioritize Like A Pro

Alright, so you've sat down at your desk and opened up your school diary, only to notice that what appears to be written down in front of you is not so much a to-do list of homework tasks, but a list as long as the receipt from your back-to-school supplies shopping spree! When it comes to figuring out how to tackle your long list of to-do's, prioritizing your tasks is extremely important. You definitely don't want to be structuring your precious time around unnecessary or unimportant tasks; otherwise you might end up tending to that major assignment at the last minute. Prioritizing your tasks is an excellent way to ensure you allocate the majority of your time to the most important tasks and can also help you to avoid the stress and anxiety associated with last minute cramming. Using a priority matrix will also help you to stay organized and maximize your productivity by spending less time on unimportant tasks. When I was in university, I discovered the magical powers of a priority matrix and using one certainly made a huge difference to how I completed my work! While it might seem simple, it's an easy and highly effective way to get your priorities in order. Your schedule likely consists of a range of tasks that vary in their level of urgency and importance. Simply re-organize your to-do list by making note of each task's level of urgency and importance, before prioritizing tasks that fall into the urgent/important matrix.

~ Take a look at how I set out my priority matrix on the next page. How would you organize your to-do list? Use the empty priority matrix and practice organizing your list of homework for the week, according to each one's level of urgency and importance. ~

	urgent	**not urgent**
important	▷ Study for biology test on Thursday ▷ complete science project due Friday ▷ Read chapter 3 for tomorrow's English class	▷ Begin writing essay ▷ Write weekly summaries ▷ Get permission slip signed
not important	▷ Return library book	▷ Decorate my new school diary

	urgent	**not urgent**
important		
not important		

Winding Up Your Study Sessions

How you finish studying is just as important as how you start. Do you ever find yourself half way through completing a piece of homework, or a few pages into your weekly readings as you reach the end of your study session? It can be frustrating to have to stop studying abruptly so that you don't risk going overtime and neglecting your other responsibilities. Instead, as you approach the end of your study session, use the last five to ten minutes to start winding things up. This is your time to review what work you managed to complete, before making a note of any remaining tasks that you need to come back to the following day. Doing so, will help you to ease out of your study session and also help you pick up where you left off when you next come back to your desk!

My Top 5 Tips
For Structuring Your Study Sessions

 Study during your peak energy periods of the day to maximize your productivity.

 Study for twenty-five to thirty minutes at a time.

 Take a five to ten minute break in between each study session to help you stay focused and avoid feeling tired or restless.

 Use a priority matrix to help focus your attention on important tasks.

 Use the final five to ten minutes of your study sessions to wind up and make a list of anything that you still need to complete.

The Art of Effective Goal Setting

If you look around my study, you will most definitely see that I am a big believer in goal setting! Hanging on my wall behind my desk, you'll find a large vision board where I display my goals for each month, as well as goals that I aim to accomplish in the not too distant future. Whenever there is something I want to achieve, I always make sure to write it down, remind myself of its importance on a daily basis and make a plan for how I am going to achieve it. After all, isn't a goal without a plan just a dream? Apart from these goals there is something else written at the top of my board, but I'll get to that in a moment...

I've always set myself goals, however writing them down and making a plan of attack was only something that I started doing in my final years of studying. One week in class, my psychology teacher went off on a tangent and started talking to us about the benefits of goal setting. I think she felt the need to give us a brief rundown on the matter, because she noticed some of us were having a hard time staying motivated and on track with our studies. Apart from educating us on the importance of setting short-term goals every time we sat down at our desk to study, she mentioned another type of goal – something that stuck with me ever since. It was the idea of thinking up a big picture goal and becoming consciously aware of why it was that we were even taking her class and studying in the first place. Ok, so maybe some of us were there because the thought of dropping out of school would have given our parents a heart attack, although there had to be another reason. For myself at least, I knew that there needed to be a deeper meaning behind why I chose to come to class every day and put in the hours of hard work and dedication.

Her question sat with me for the rest of the afternoon as I kept thinking about why I was working so hard and putting so much pressure on myself. There had to be a reason and there was! I wanted to get into the psychology course at one of the top universities in the state, because what I really wanted was to help make a positive change in people's lives. I wanted to contribute back to society and I thought that a career in psychology would give my life meaning and purpose. That was why I was working so hard. That was the reason for all of the countless hours of studying that I had been putting in over the years. It was only when I recognized this that my perception of my time at school changed and I was able to redirect my energy towards something that was positive, empowering and meaningful – certainly more empowering and meaningful than the grades that appear at the top of a page!

To this day I always make sure to have my big picture goal written down somewhere I can see it. I used to write it down on a sticky note and place it underneath the keyboard of my laptop so that every time I sat down to work I would be reminded to channel my efforts to something meaningful. Now, I keep it written in the top right hand corner of my vision board so I never lose sight of what is truly important. I have my short-term goals, the things I want to accomplish each month, but I always remind myself of the purpose behind them and why it's so important that I do achieve them.

Benefits Of Goal Setting

Do you ever feel yourself lacking the motivation to sit down at your desk and study? Have you ever caught yourself getting off track and feel that your study sessions could do with more structure? Perhaps you are left feeling stressed by the weight of pressure you place on yourself and have lost sight of why you are studying in the first place? If you're in search of a remedy to any of these problems then you're in luck! Goal setting is an effective and powerful tool to help you stay on track and make sure you don't lose sight of what you want in your life. What's more, setting yourself goals is an excellent way to boost your motivation and increase your productivity during your study sessions!

The Different Types Of Goals

 Short-term vs. Long-term goals

There are two main types of goals that often get a mention when discussing the benefits and methods of effective goal setting: short-term goals and long-term goals. Whilst they differ significantly from one another, both have their own unique benefits that can help to bring about success. Setting yourself short-term goals on a daily basis helps to provide you with some much-needed direction and can be used to keep you on track with your homework and assignments. Whenever I used to sit down to study, I would write myself several goals that I wanted to achieve by the end of my study sessions. This would help me to stay focused on the tasks at hand and motivate me to get my work done so that I could experience the joy of crossing them off my to-do list that night! Short-term goals do not however need to be things that you want to accomplish that day. Although not set in stone, usually their timeline stretches anywhere from a day to a couple of months. If your short-term goals happen to be on the longer end of the time frame, then it can be useful to break them down further. Compartmentalizing your goals creates an achievable plan so that you can execute them effectively!

On the other hand, long-term goals refer to major milestones or important achievements that you set out to accomplish further down the track, such as over the next year. These are the sort of goals that require not only more time, but also a lot more planning. Breaking these goals down and identifying the smaller tasks or requirements that must first be completed is highly important. You'll likely find that you come up with a number of tasks, so it's useful to create a timeline and set yourself clear and realistic deadlines for when you aim to achieve each goal. This allows you to track your progress and can also act as a motivator because let's face it, if you're setting out to achieve a goal that takes a year or sometimes longer to complete, you will probably need some reinforcement along the way! For example, when I was in high school, I decided that I wanted to study psychology in university. Being a long-term goal, I realized that there were several requirements that had to be met in order for me to achieve this. I would need to choose the appropriate subjects in my final years of school, be successful in my final exams, apply for the course, and then be accepted by the university I had applied to. All of these steps took time, dedication and determination, and each could be broken down even further. If I wouldn't have broken my long-term goal into smaller achievements, it certainly would have been easy to lose sight of my end goal and it's importance. Perhaps I might have even given up?

Unlike short-term and long-term goals that are designed to help keep you focused and on track, big picture goals tend to bring about a sense of purpose and act as a reminder for why you are working so hard in the first place. They are often intertwined with your purpose or something more meaningful you want out of life. Having a big picture goal encourages you to consider what you want out of your future and even how you would like to contribute to society. It can often help to be reminded that as you complete each assignment and exam, you inch yourself closer to your big picture goal.

When it comes to being a student and trying to figure out the real driving force behind all those late nights of studying, the best place to start is with a simple yet powerful question: "Why is my education important to me?" Take some time to really consider what you intend to gain from your studies. Then, when all of those assignments start to pile up, the workload begins to seem overwhelming or you find yourself starting to doubt in your abilities, reminding yourself of why you are committed to your studies can help to reignite that spark of determination and re-establish a sense of purpose. Write it down and pin it on a vision board, stick it on your laptop or place it inside your school diary. Wherever you choose to display it, allow it to be your constant reminder to help guide you through the haze that forms in the presence of the busy and sometimes hectic school year.

My Short-Term Goals

Have a think about three short-term goals you want to accomplish this school year and write them down in the spaces below.

1 ....

2 ....

3 ....

When do you plan on achieving these goals?

I plan to achieve goal #1 by: ....

I plan to achieve goal #2 by: ....

I plan to achieve goal #3 by: ....

My Long-Term Goals

Use the space below to write down a long-term goal for this year. What do you want to achieve?

My goal for this year is to

. . . .

When do you plan on achieving this goal?

I plan to achieve this goal by . . . .

Now break down your long-term goal into smaller goals. What steps must you first complete in order to achieve this goal?

Step 1. . . . .

I aim to achieve this by . . . .

Step 2. ---

I aim to achieve this by -----------------------

Step 3. ---

I aim to achieve this by -----------------------

Step 4. ---

I aim to achieve this by -----------------------

Step 5. ---

I aim to achieve this by -----------------------

My Big Picture Goal

Take some time to now think about your big picture
goal. Consider why you value your education and what
you intend to gain from your studies. Perhaps you have
a particular career pathway in mind?

In the future, I want to -----------------------

My Top 5 Tips
For Setting Goals

 Always write down your goals to increase the likelihood of committing to them and taking action!

 Set yourself short-term goals to boost your productivity and keep you focused on the tasks at hand.

 Break down larger goals to help you create an achievable plan of attack.

 Create a timeline with realistic deadlines for when you plan to achieve you goals.

 Display your goals around your room to remind yourself of them daily.

Staying Focused In Class

was always a conscientious student. Some might have even called me a teachers' pet. It wasn't as if I spent my spare time completing every piece of extra credit work I could get my hands on, but I was definitely one of those students who was known to sit up straight, chin up, hands resting and clasped together on the desk, ready to be called on by the teacher at any time. You could usually find me seated in the front row, eyes and ears wide open, brain ticking, hands ready and waiting to shoot up into the sky to answer a question. I always made an effort to participate in class, to do my best to answer questions and also ask questions of my own when a topic was unclear. Let me make it clear though I go any further that I was not one of those students who would hog the teacher's attention and try to answer every question that was posed to the class. I promise I knew when to hold back and rarely, okay, only sometimes did I have to be told to give the other students a chance and stop raising my hand!

Not surprisingly, my tendency to immerse myself in my classes carried through to my years of studying at university. Just like I used to in school, I would make sure to get to class early and grab a seat in the front row. I did however run late to class one day and ended up sitting closer to the back of the lecture theatre, gazing over the rest of my classmates. It was actually quite funny to catch a glimpse of what I probably looked like. There in front of me was a line of MacBook laptops, intermittently connected to pairs of quick moving hands, eagerly taking down the lecturer's words of wisdom. Yep, I had gone from sporting pigtails in school to wearing converse sneakers in university, though my diligence and multiple hand raises in class remained.

Dealing With Distractions

Being able to concentrate for the duration of your class can be challenging. There are often a number of distractions that begin to tempt your focus and leave you itching for the school bell to ring! Not everyone finds it easy to sit for long periods of time without losing focus. In fact, despite my conscientious reputation, I myself am not a stranger to repeated clock staring! If I'm going to discuss how to stay focused in class then I'd first better set the scene! Picture this: You're seated near the window - the portal to the outside world where freedom awaits you. Evidently, you start staring out onto the playground and wishing it were lunchtime again. You shift your gaze back to the front of the room where there's another student one row in front of you. She keeps playing with her ponytail, trying to smooth out any bumps and making sure no piece is left astray. Her ponytail swishes from side to side, hypnotizing you like a pendulum. At the same time, two students in the back row keep leaning up against the wall on their chairs, until, lo and behold, one of them finally falls off, forcing all of the students to turn around in a burst of laughter. To make matters worse, your pencil case is now beginning to resemble a comfy resting place for your head, since you opted to stay up late last night to binge watch your new favorite show. How are you supposed to pay attention with all of these distractions going on? Now your focus has drifted from the board to a loose thread on your jumper and the silent conversation you begin to have with yourself sounds a little something like this:

"What did he just say? I zoned out for a good few minutes there! How much longer until class finishes? Argh, maybe if this teacher's voice was not so monotonous, I would actually be able to follow what he is saying... What are those boys doing over there? They are going to get in trouble if they keep that up. Seriously, why can't everyone just be quiet and stop distracting me?!"

The Common Causes

While there are many distractions that have the ability to lead your focus astray in the classroom, for every problem there is a viable solution! It's simply a matter of becoming aware of what is likely to hinder your ability to pay attention in class, so that you can then act on them, either by avoiding the distractions all together or taking action to stop them from interfering with your learning.

 Shhh! Stop Talking!

They say it's always easiest to blame others for our problems, so let's start with those chatty classmates! If only there was a mute button to cancel out all of the noise and chatter in the room that keeps pulling your focus from what is most important! I'd sure love to get my hands on one of those kinds of remote controls if they are ever made! I'm sure I would have put it to good use, aiming it at all of the students that used to use our math lessons as their chance to discuss last night's TV shows or schedule their weekend plans.

Nowadays, I would probably use it on my neighbor's dog that enjoys communicating with his friends across the street, as well as warning potential intruders as they walk past in a hurry. Did I mention that his body clock wakes him up with the urge to bark as early as sunrise? His conversations certainly make writing a book a little challenging! Anyway, where was I? I guess I got distracted and veered off on a tangent... Oh, that's right: chatty classmates!

You may not like what I am about to say, however sitting next to your friends is a common reason for getting distracted in class. Perhaps you and your 'bff' have the tendency to pass notes, text each other under the table or communicate silently through secret hand gestures to avoid getting called out by the teacher.

In these circumstances, I highly recommend sitting apart and saving your recess and lunchtime breaks for your catch-ups. If it's the rest of your peers that keep distracting you with their side conversations and antics, then there are a few ways to manage the problem. First off, it's worthwhile to try and sit as far away as possible from these students. It can be challenging to not let yourself be curious about what others are talking about or doing when they are sitting right behind you!

I always preferred to sit up the front and near the teacher because it put these students out of sight and I was more likely to focus on what was going on right in front of me – mainly, what my teacher was saying. Sometimes, you might find that the problem persists and your classmates' chatter becomes a regular and annoying occurrence.

In this case, it can be a good idea to bring their attention to their behaviour and let them know it is distracting you from focusing in class. A simple; "Please try and keep it down. It's hard to concentrate when you keep talking," ought to do it. If anything, they should be understanding of your needs, considering class time is meant to be for learning and not for side chitchat.

If you feel uncomfortable or worry about a conflict arising, another option is to let your teacher be the 'bad guy.' Make sure to tell your teacher that the behaviour of your classmates is distracting you and stopping you for learning in class.

If your teacher was unaware at first, you can be certain your peers' background noise won't go unnoticed for much longer! Hopefully, your teacher will handle the situation next time it arises and you will be able to return to a distraction free zone. Well, almost... Did I mention there are a whole bunch of other distractions we still have to cover?

 I'm Hungry!

Have you heard of three-thirtyitis? Perhaps you've experienced your energy levels spike and fall throughout the day? Feeling tired as the afternoon approaches is another reason for having trouble staying focused in class. The most common cause behind the lack of energy we experience in the early afternoon is due to a drop in our blood sugar levels. Not surprisingly, the fastest and most effective cure is food – healthy food of course!

Many people already understand the science behind the lack of energy that we no doubt experience several hours after lunchtime, however what about those of us who feel as though we are trapped in time, re-living this moment all day long?! If your bowl of brightly colored cereal is not getting you through first period, take it as a sign that you need to re-evaluate your meal choices. Remember, food is fuel! Foods containing high levels of sugar and processed ingredients leave your body feeling unsatisfied, result in a short lasting energy spike and can negatively impact your brain's ability to function optimally.

In contrast, eating foods high in antioxidants, rich in protein and omega-3 fatty acids, as well as those that have a low GI can help you to better sustain your energy levels throughout the day and provide your body with the necessary fuel it requires to function at its best!

 I'm Restless!

What about those moments when you just can't sit still and find yourself itching for any excuse to leave the classroom? I bet that a quick bathroom break or even being asked to run an errand for the teacher sure sounds pretty good right about now... It's normal to need to get up and stretch after a while. In fact, it's actually quite unnatural for us to expect our bodies to be able to sit still for long periods of time.

If switching positions in your seat isn't doing it for you, try asking your teacher if you can grab a drink of water or take a quick bathroom break. Some teachers are pretty strict, while others tend to be more lenient with granting a short break. Just make sure not to abuse their good nature or their patience will likely begin to wear thin!

If you don't happen to be so lucky and you, along with your classmates are trapped for the next little while, make sure to use your breaks wisely. Rather than spending your recess and lunchtime sitting around with friends, opt for a short walk around campus and talk on the go. You don't necessarily need to break out a sweat! Any form of light exercise will help to combat feelings of restlessness and clear your mind so that you are ready to head back to class.

 I Don't Care!

The last factor on my list is not so much a distraction in itself, but something that can often lead you to zone out during class and lose focus. It has the potential to impact the quality of your overall learning and is probably the most important ingredient for staying focused in class!

Can you guess what it is? If you guessed participating in class then you're spot on! It's understandable that not every topic you learn in class will interest you or seem like a relevant prerequisite for your desired career choice. Nonetheless, sitting quietly and daydreaming about what you plan on doing over summer break won't do you any good.

In fact, it will only make time appear to move more slowly. Much to some students' dismay, class attendance is not enough! Try to be an active class participant, contributing to class discussions and asking questions where possible.

Of course, you aren't expected to raise your hand at every chance or know the answers to every question. Simply look for opportunities to speak up and in doing so you will be enriching your learning experience.

Being prepared for class will certainly help you here as well, since completing your homework and weekly readings will enable you to follow your teacher's lesson plan and feel confident to get involved. Importantly, the more involved you are, the less likely you are to lose focus and begin looking for alternative stimuli around the classroom!

My Top 5 Tips
For Staying Focused In Class

 Avoid sitting next to students who are likely going to distract you.

 Notify a teacher if your classmates continue to distract you from learning.

 Maintain a healthy diet and eat substantial meals to help sustain your energy levels throughout the day.

 Combat feeling restless by using your recess and lunchtime breaks to be physically active.

 Be an active class participant by contributing towards class discussions and asking questions.

Think :) Positive!

This may come as a surprise to you but I like to be prepared. I know, shocker, right? Aside from stating the obvious, something that you may not know about me is that while I like to be prepared when it comes to my work, I also have a tendency to try and prepare for anything and everything that life throws at me. If I could, and trust me I have tried, I would want to know exactly what my future holds. The problem here is that the only thing one can ever be sure of is that nothing in life is certain – well, except for death and taxes, although that does sound pretty morbid! While I liked to think that I knew exactly how my life would pan out since I was a teenager; what profession I would have or even what age I would get married, I really had no idea... Let's just say I would make the worst fortune teller!

It's taken me a while and having to live in my stubborn, impatient and somewhat undisciplined mind certainly hasn't made it any easier. I have however finally come to terms with the fact that the universe has something else planned for me. It takes a clear vision, hard work, and faith, but as long as I stay true to myself, I am comforted knowing that things have a way of working themselves out. If only this pattern of thinking was something I could have adopted earlier on in life. Instead, my need to feel in control and prepared for whatever was around the corner meant I also had a tendency to engage in internal 'worst case scenario' brainstorming sessions. It's easy to allow our minds to run straight to the negative possibilities as opposed to focusing on all of the positive outcomes that are likely to happen. It's as though we engage in damage control before any damage has even occurred! Perhaps it's a way to help cushion the fall in the event that there ever is one... This detrimental thinking however, did not do me any good. In fact, my 'what if?' mindset only made studying for exams and completing assignments more challenging - as though they weren't already difficult enough! I distinctly remember sitting down at my allocated desk in the school hall to take my final psychology exam and saying to myself "what if I don't get an A on my exam?" Then, with a few minutes to spare at the end, I remember flipping through the exam booklet attempting to see how many questions I could possibly have answered incorrectly and trying to see what was the worst possible score I could expect. I know it sounds crazy, at least to me it does, especially as I sit here and think back on my past behaviours!

The truth is, I don't remember there ever being a specific turning point in my life that helped me climb out of this negative thought pattern. I think it was a combination of pep talks, yoga workshops, the odd self-help book and maturity that collectively helped to change my mindset. Of course nobody is perfect and once in a while I still catch myself out with my negative thinking, however I try to remind myself to think positively and attract more of what I want in my life. I know that having a positive mindset and freeing myself of catastrophic thinking patterns plays a significant role in life's outcomes. How can one possibly try to prepare for the worst yet simultaneously still hope for the best? I equate this inconsistency with tying yourself to a poll and still expecting to fly. If you truly want to soar, you'll have to untie yourself and simply let go.

Delightfully Difficult

Your perception of your studies as well as your own capabilities is an important factor that can influence your overall academic performance. That's right, getting good grades requires more than hard work! It requires a positive mindset and the right kind of attitude. When I was in school I used to think that grades were independent of your mindset and that thinking positively was by no means going to help me read my textbook faster, remember important definitions or make complicated math equations any easier to solve. While thinking positive won't give you super fast reading powers or a photographic memory, it does change how you approach your studies and can also give you the confidence boost you need to persevere and keep trying until you successfully reach your goals. I like to use the oxymoron 'delightfully difficult' to prove my point! What I mean here is; do you see a complicated task as a problem or as a challenge that you are willing to rise up to? Seeing something in a positive light or as 'delightfully difficult' helps to create a solution focused mindset and your perception of the task begins to change. Importantly, how you perceive something and the way you choose to label it has the ability to impact the end result – in this case, your grades.

You Can Do It!

The same applies to how you perceive yourself and your own abilities. It's important to keep a positive perception, seeing yourself as capable and focusing on your past successes as opposed to 'failures.' Ask yourself: "How do I see myself? What sort of student do I perceive myself to be?" One thing that I will mention here is that confidence is key! When you have confidence in your abilities it will ultimately help to erode much of the stress and anxiety experienced around studying. This is because perceiving the outcome as being out of our control can cause these types of emotions to surface. That being said, if you are confident in your ability to study for a test effectively, if you remind yourself of times when you did well in class or successfully completed exams, then you will likely feel more in control of your studies and adopt a 'can-do' attitude!

Positive Self-Talk

Your perception of yourself is closely linked to the way you talk to yourself. Don't worry, I am not referring to those moments when you catch yourself thinking out loud, only for a family member to walk into your room and look at you strangely! I am talking about the voice inside your head that tells you whether you are good enough (hint: you are!), if you should keep trying or simply give up. This self-talk that we frequently engage in has the ability to really shape our confidence and influence how we approach a situation. To put this into perspective, try and picture yourself sitting an exam and being faced with a question that you cannot seem to answer. As you stare at the question with a puzzled look on your face you can hear a voice in your ear saying the following: "The question hasn't been covered in class at all and is part of the exam to taunt you. You can't possibly know the answer! You might be smart enough to get the first few questions correct but this one is much harder and will take you ages to solve... if you ever get there that is!" Let me ask you this: do you think it would be appropriate for someone to say these sorts of things to you while you are trying to complete an exam? No? Then why tell yourself such things? Looking at the question with even a grain of self-doubt can create a defeatist attitude and make you want to give up.

What if, instead of those negative statements, that voice begins to give you a pep talk? "You managed to solve the previous few questions, so there's no reason you can't solve this one too! Just because you didn't see this exact question in class, doesn't mean you can't apply your knowledge and find the answer!" Hearing these sorts of remarks, wouldn't you then be more inclined to keep going, perceiving the answer as being within arm's reach? Even though that little voice didn't give you the answer, the way you approach each question can significantly impact your ability to solve it. With this in mind, take your studies as an opportunity for growth and development. Rise up to the challenges and observe how you instantly, and somewhat subconsciously are able to see a task as more manageable and as having an achievable solution.

~ Cut out the positive palm cards on the following page, in addition to making your own. Keep them on your desk, in your pocket or school bag and read over them regularly to help create a positive mindset! ~

I EMBRACE NEW CHALLENGES
AS OPPORTUNITIES TO LEARN
AND ACQUIRE NEW SKILLS.

EVERY SUBJECT HAS
SOMETHING VALUABLE
TO TEACH ME. I COME TO
CLASS WITH AN OPEN MIND
AND AM READY TO LEARN!

I AM CONFIDENT IN MY ABILITIES
TO SUCCEED IN SCHOOL. I WORK
HARD AND MY EFFORTS ARE REWARDED.

I ENJOY GOING TO SCHOOL. MY TEACHERS
AND FRIENDS SUPPORT ME AND HELP TO
CREATE A POSITIVE EXPERIENCE.

My Top 5 Tips
For Staying Positive

 View complicated tasks as a challenge that you are willing to rise up to.

 Focus on your past successes instead of failures.

 Maintain a positive perception of yourself and your abilities.

 Avoid catastrophic thinking.

 Engage in positive self-talk. Say to yourself: "I can do this!"

Tackling Major Assignments

Perhaps I'm not supposed to tell you this, seeing as my purpose is to instill in you a love for learning, however I used to really dislike reading! While I now enjoy curling up on the couch with a cup of tea, a blanket and a good book, my love for reading only blossomed over the past few years. I guess I never found the right sort of books to suit my interests – that, and I was too stubborn and impatient to give a book a real chance! My parents used to have to bribe me with fashion magazines in the hopes that I would do more than just flip through the pages and glance at the photographs of models wearing the latest trends for the upcoming season. Even as I started studying at university I still could not be tempted by some of the most popular novels of the year. I spent so much time reading textbooks and dozens of articles, researching for my assignments and final thesis, that to then occupy myself in my spare time by reading even more was unappealing to say the least!

Being the stubborn teenager that I was, my refusal to read in my spare time eventually got me into a little trouble. In middle school, my grade eight English teacher decided that our major assignment for the semester would be to write a book report. "You may choose to write your reports on any of the books you have read recently and thoroughly enjoyed!" she said. Well, considering I hadn't read any books that semester besides my textbooks, I either had to find a book and get reading, or opt for a different approach entirely. Of course, I chose the latter! Even though I didn't enjoy reading, I was very fond of creative writing, so I decided to conjure up a story that would have made for an interesting book. Besides, my teacher couldn't possibly have known of every book that was ever written, so making one up seemed like a plan! My storyline was well thought out; there were interesting characters, unforeseen drama and a clear and appropriate ending. It was as though I was watching the whole story play out right in front of me! With my storyline in place, I began writing my book report and handed it in the following week. So how did I go in the end? Well, believe it or not I got an A+! My teacher loved the report so much that she was compelled to tell my mother about my work in the staffroom one morning. Oh, that's right, I forgot to mention that my mother worked at my school... I'm sure you can guess what happened next! My mother, thinking it wouldn't be an issue, told my teacher that I made the whole thing up! Maybe it wasn't the smartest idea to have let my mother in on my secret plan after all? Luckily, the repercussions were not all that bad and the two of them ended up having a good laugh at my expense. I did however learn my lesson and vowed not to try and skimp out by taking shortcuts when it came to doing my next assignment!

Stage 1 - Planning Your Approach

Before getting into the particular types of assignments that you will need to complete during high school, I thought I'd better first focus on the importance of having the right approach! Planning how you aim to tackle major assignments will help you deal with the increasing workload that comes with being in high school. Naturally, the thought of having to complete a major assignment for class can feel overwhelming, so it's important to remember that every assignment is made up of smaller parts or tasks. Instead of focusing on the assignment as a whole, try and focus on each task individually. This can make the assignment seem a lot more manageable as it assists you to direct your attention and concentrate on one part of the assignment at a time. Surprisingly, this is not something that I learned at school, but rather something that my grandmother taught me a few years ago. I remember one afternoon paying her a visit, while feeling stressed about my thesis. Once I told her the source of my stress, she looked at me and asked, "Jessica, do you know how you eat an elephant?" In that moment I knew that she was about to pass on some of her words of wisdom and I was right. The answer to her question was simple, yet powerful. It was; "one bite at a time." Her advice taught me that no task, project or goal in life is too big, as long as you take it one step at a time.

Stage 2 - **Researching The Topic**

When it comes to actually tackling your major assignments and projects, this one tip can make a huge difference to the quality of work that you produce! Although it may sound tedious, try to research your topic thoroughly for a few days before starting your assignment. Now when I say 'research your topic', I don't mean that you should briefly skim over your class notes. Instead, try and rely on multiple resources, such as textbooks, relevant articles and websites, in addition to your notes from class. Putting in the extra effort early on will ensure that you have a good grasp of the topic and help you decide how to best plan out your assignment. This can also help ensure that your assignment covers all of the necessary information that your teacher is looking for and most importantly - grading you on!

Essay Writing

The first kind of major assignment that is all too familiar during high school and college or university is essay writing! All right, so maybe it's not everyone's favorite way to spend precious time afterschool... It is however something that you will encounter every year, so it's important to try and get the hang of crafting those essays early on. Writing a comprehensive essay that is well thought out, structured and flows logically takes time. Instead of delving straight into the essay, it's important to carefully consider and plan your response, so that your point of view is effectively conveyed throughout your writing.

 Planning Your Response

When setting out to plan your essay, make sure that you first understand your essay topic. I recommend taking a pen and underlining the key terms and phrases in your essay topic to ensure you answer the question appropriately. Make sure to pay close attention to any task or instruction words that appear in the essay question such as "discuss, explain, or compare." These words are there to guide how you should approach the essay, so it's especially important to take note of these! You certainly don't want to spend hours on your paper only to receive a poor grade because your response was not appropriately tailored to the question! Once you have understood what the question is asking, it's time to get planning. Although it may change depending on the type of paper you are assigned, one way to help you plan your essay is to adopt the 5-paragraph structure. This framework takes on a formulaic approach to essay writing and is comprised of an introduction paragraph, three body paragraphs and a conclusion paragraph.

The 5-Paragraph Structure

◦ Introduction

Try and think of this paragraph as a little summary of your paper that draws your reader in from the start. Make sure to address the essay question right from the beginning of your paper to ensure you get off to a strong start and avoid getting off track! Consider starting your essay with an attention-grabbing opening sentence, before providing some broad background information about the topic, such as a brief outline and even including relevant statistics and data. As you progress further into the Introduction paragraph, it is important to mention how you plan on addressing the essay question. That's right, all of your hard work and hours spent researching your topic are about to finally pay off! It is at this point that you should introduce the main points that will be discussed in more detail throughout each of your body paragraphs. These points should essentially reflect the angle you have chosen to take in your writing, as their role is to support the backbone of your essay - your argument. Providing a brief outline of your main points also sets the scene for you to then clearly state your overall contention, which is typically written out as your 'thesis statement' and referred back to several times throughout your essay.

° Body Paragraphs

When writing your body paragraphs, start by selecting three main points or ideas that support your argument and discuss each one in depth. Although each of your ideas will complement one another and collectively build on your argument, they are still viewed as independent and therefore should be organized into separate body paragraphs. Dividing them up will help bring more structure to your writing and allow the reader to focus on one idea at a time. Importantly, when writing your body paragraphs, each one should:

1. Demonstrate how it relates to the previous paragraph.

2. Begin with a topic sentence.

3. Include supporting evidence for each point.

4. Emphasize how the essay question is being addressed.

° Conclusion

And finally we are up to the Conclusion! This paragraph is where you should restate your overall contention or 'thesis statement', in order to draw the body of the essay together. When creating your Conclusion, and I cannot stress this enough as someone who has both written and marked many essays during university, make sure you do not include any new information. This section of your essay is there to summarize the most important points that you have already discussed, so that you can showcase how you have proven your argument. After all, the aim of the Conclusion is to convince the reader that your essay has covered the most important information needed to effectively address the topic. Make sure that you spend some time carefully crafting this final paragraph, as it is going to leave the reader with a lasting impression of your work. That being said, although your motivation may begin to decrease by this point, it is really important not to rush through this section, because you don't want any of your hard work to go to waste!

Oral Presentations

Considering my love of performing, this next form of assignment happens to be my favorite! There was one year when my English teacher told us that as part of our requirements for our oral presentation, we were to embody a character from a book we had been studying in class. I was so determined to get into character and convey the sad story of a girl who had been taken from her family, that right before I got up to present, I put vapor rub right underneath my eyes – you know, the ointment you put on your chest when you have a cold! Needless to say, my teacher and classmates were very impressed with my ability to cry on command and said that my presentation was not only powerful, but also highly memorable! Come to think of it, I wonder if my efforts to get good grades were a little bit excessive?

While oral presentations were something that I used to look forward to in school, many students dread the thought of having to stand up and present in front of their classmates. In fact, I once heard that more people are scared of giving a speech in public than they are of death itself! If you ask me, that's a whole lot of fear to be carrying for so many years of our lives! Don't get me wrong; I still feel those butterflies forming in my stomach no matter how many times I have given a speech in public! The difference is that rather than hindering my performance, these nerves help to prepare me by getting me excited to go up on stage and present in front of a crowd. Whether you notice your heart beginning to race or you happen to feel quite comfortable, there are a number of factors that collectively contribute towards the overall quality of your presentation and can help to earn you a high mark.

 Engage With The Audience

This first pointer can be the difference between maintaining your audience's focus and losing them halfway through your speech! Do you ever watch talk show hosts and find yourself getting lost in their words? They have a way of skilfully drawing their audience in and capturing their attention. When it comes to giving a presentation in class, the same principles of engaging with your audience apply. Engaging with your audience does not necessarily mean that you have to give a funny or entertaining speech. You are not expected to get your classmates up out of their chairs and dancing like you see on Ellen! Rather, you could begin your speech with a question or talk directly to your audience members, instructing them to think about a particular scenario or carry out a task. Engaging with your audience will make your presentation more entertaining, interesting and interactive. Another advantage is that as you begin to involve your audience in your presentation, you will also likely begin to feel more relaxed and enjoy presenting in front of your peers!

 ## Be Mindful Of Your Body

Another way to engage with your audience and make your presentation captivating is to use body language. Eye contact and hand gestures are key to giving an engaging speech! Try to maintain eye contact with your audience and use appropriate body language to help convey your points. Be aware of your body and notice whether you tend to sway from side to side or stand completely still when you begin to feel nervous. Trust me, there is nothing more uncomfortable as an audience member than watching the presenter appear nervous or uptight!

 ## Relax

One way to help combat feelings of anxiety is to allow yourself to take at least one mindful breath before you commence your presentation. You are allowed to take a moment to gather your thoughts, and in doing so, you will be able to start off with a clear and focused mind. If you begin to feel overwhelmed by the thought of having to present to a classroom full of students, try to treat your presentation as a group discussion or conversation. This is your chance to state your case and share your thoughts, opinions and knowledge about a topic. Remember, no one is there to judge you and you are all in the exact same boat – even if sometimes it may feel like that boat has sailed out onto rough and unchartered waters!

 Use Cards As A Guide

To make things a little easier on yourself, most teachers will also allow or suggest that you have your speech on a set of palm cards while you present. Palm card are a fantastic cue, however I do remember some of my classmates reading their speeches off their palm cards word-for-word. Palm cards are excellent for helping you stay on track and remember important points to address, however they are there to be used only as a guide and not to excuse you from learning your speech! Try including dot points rather than your entire speech, so that they can be used to jog your memory and still enable you to maintain eye contact with your audience.

 Practice Makes Perfect

My final suggestion to help you deliver a strong presentation in class is one that ties in with managing those little butterflies in your stomach that sometimes transform into stomping elephants... You have no doubt spent time writing an excellent speech, so make sure to set aside several days to rehearse. Consider practicing in front of a mirror, recording yourself, and presenting in front of family members. Rehearsing your speech in front of others will not only help to effectively consolidate your speech into your long term memory, it will also help you become more accustomed to presenting in front of crowds. After all, the more familiar you are with your speech, the less likely you are to feel nervous and stumble.

Group Projects

The last form of assignment is one that can be quite challenging, not because of the work itself, but because it requires teamwork - sometimes with team members who have less motivation than others. When I was studying, I enjoyed working with other classmates - provided we could choose our group members, that is! Unfortunately, we can't always get our way and there is the possibility that you may end up being assigned to work with students who either have a tendency to take control, or attempt to pawn off their work to the rest of the group. I remember a few group projects where some team members would try and take credit for all of the hard work that the rest of the group members and I had done! To save you the struggles of trying to be reassigned to another group, there are other, more useful strategies that can help make working in groups a lot more manageable. Besides, working in teams is often something that future employers will require you to do, so it's important that you learn how to work with even the most difficult of people!

 Be Willing to Share

Often, confrontation between group members can arise when people begin to feel as though their ideas are not being acknowledged. Each group member has something valuable to contribute, so make sure to allow and encourage everyone to share ideas at the start. Consider having a small brainstorming session where each person can put forward his or her suggestions. While not every idea will seem appropriate, this phase is there to stimulate ideas and get everyone's minds thinking. There have been many times when I have entered a brainstorming session with other people and although not every suggestion was used, some did spark some inspiration and lead to great ideas! Of course, not all ideas will seem appropriate or viable, which means compromise between group members is key!

 Establish Your Roles

Once you have come to a general consensus of what your group plans to do for the assignment, create a list of the various tasks that need to be completed. It's important to make sure that everyone in your group knows exactly what his or her responsibilities are from the very beginning. This way, you can relax knowing that everyone is ready and willing to share the workload and that there is no reason for one person to bear the weight of the assignment all on their own. Just make sure to also set clear deadlines so that everything gets done on time! Consider also appointing one person to take on the role of 'group leader' in addition to other responsibilities. This person is in charge of organizing and holding meet-ups and collating the final work from each group member. They will therefore need to make sure that they obtain everyone's contact details at the beginning and circulate these around the group. It's also important that this person does not view themselves as the boss of the group, but that their role is to make sure that everything goes according to plan.

The Final Stage

It can be easy to forget this final step, however it's really important to reward yourself for all of your hard work! Whatever the type of assignment happens to be, make sure to reward yourself and give yourself something to look forward to. Have a think about something you can do to spoil yourself, whether it is going out with your friends, seeing a movie, going shopping or attending a special event. You deserve a break, so set aside some time for yourself once you have completed your assignment!

My Top 5 Tips
For Completing Assignments

 Break down your major assignments into smaller tasks.

 Set clear deadlines for when you aim to complete each task.

 Research your topic thoroughly for a few days before starting your assignment.

 Rely on multiple resources when researching your topic.

 Remember to reward yourself after you complete your assignment!

Dealing

With

Disappointment

was always an impatient student when it came time to get my results back for an assignment or exam. From the moment I had submitted my work, I would eagerly anticipate getting my grade back. While I did have confidence that I had given my best effort and satisfied the assessment criteria, there were times when my grades did not align with my expectations. It was in these instances that I would feel the weight of the world fall onto my shoulders. An unwelcomed sense of hopelessness would emerge and was usually accompanied by its partner in crime - self-doubt. Despite my positive outlook on life, I would occasionally throw myself a short-lasting pity party, however after the party was over, I was always determined to improve in my studies and made an effort and promise to myself to "do better next time!"

My disappointment in receiving lower than expected grades contrasted with the extreme excitement that would follow in the event of a perfect score. I remember one of my best friend's parents used to reward her for getting 100% on her assignments and exams by taking her out for ice cream that night. I on the other hand, rewarded myself with a secret little happy dance – well that, and a burning desire to continue my winning streak! I loved the idea of having a perfect score so much that I wanted to hold onto it for as long as I possibly could! One afternoon I remember coming home after receiving my statistics assignment back. My sister, eagerly waiting at the kitchen table asked me how I went. I was so excited to tell her that I had received a perfect score: 100/100! When I told her however, she didn't seem to share my excitement. In fact, she looked at me as though what I had said was absurd! Looking back, her reaction was fitting, particularly since there was a little more to my response than just my grade. "I got 100%, so now I need to get 100% on my class test next month because I don't want to lose my average," I remember telling her. Come to think of it, I probably wouldn't have shared my excitement at such a response either! Unsurprisingly, I did not finish the semester with a perfect average, although I did manage to get 100% on my class test the following month. That's not to say I wasn't proud of my overall performance at the end of the semester. Actually, it taught me the valuable lesson: that perfection is unsustainable and that it's much better to aim for excellence instead!

Perfectly Imperfect

Perfection is a dangerous goal to set. It creates unrealistic expectations that rob us from noticing and enjoying our achievements. It sets us up for disappointment and does no favors when it comes to staying optimistic and motivating us to persevere and try harder next time. A perfect score is absolutely something to be proud of, however writing an assignment or completing an exam with the intention of getting 100% is not a good idea. I am a firm believer in the powers of goal setting, although I don't like to think that perfection can ever be considered a realistic goal. While setting high goals can motivate and push you to achieve new heights, aiming for perfection puts an enormous amount of unnecessary pressure on yourself and unapologetically leaves no room for mistakes, or as I like to call them – areas for improvement. So why the obsession with perfection? If the expectation of a perfect score were temporarily erased from your mind, would a 99/100 not be something to be incredibly proud of? Any grade for that matter that is an improvement from your last is something to acknowledge and celebrate! The reality is that we are always learning, always growing and always working harder to be better. We are all perfectly imperfect and that is what makes life beautiful and gives us purpose to wake up each morning, knowing we are here to continue to work on ourselves.

Learning From Your Mistakes

It's easy to want to bypass all of your teacher's comments and quickly flip to the back page of your assignment to find out what grade you got. Of course, you should check what grade your teacher gave you, but more importantly you should pay close attention to your teacher's feedback. Even if you didn't do as well as you had hoped, there is no use in sulking over your grades and discarding your assignment in the trash as you allow your mind to be consumed by a cloud of disappointment and frustration. Reading your teacher's feedback is the best way to learn from your mistakes and importantly, do better next time! On the other hand, if you happen to ace an assignment, paying attention to the comments is the best way to find out and reinforce what you did right so that you can keep doing it! Now, I'll admit, I didn't always read my teacher's feedback. It only became clear to me that it was important when I noticed my grades had reached a plateau and I could not seem to improve my marks. I soon realized that those red scribbles and words written in the margin of each page were invaluable to my overall academic success. Not only would I read over the comments to try and understand where I went wrong, being the conscientious student that I was, I would also make a time to meet with my teachers after class. I found that discussing my work, and the topic in more detail, was the most effective and efficient way for me to learn from my mistakes and see fast results!

A Fixed Mindset

How you choose to look at your grades can give you an insight into how you perceive your own skills. For example, do you accept any grade that appears on your report card as an accurate representation of your overall abilities? If so, you may start to see your grades as something that is out of your control. For instance, if you perform poorly on a math test, would you say to yourself that you are no good at math? Or is it possible that you did not study for the test effectively? Perhaps you needed some extra help or did not study enough? There are numerous reasons why we don't always get the grades we would like, however it does not mean that there is no use in further trying or that we should simply give up. When it comes to your grades, having a fixed mindset won't do you any good. If anything, it will only erode your confidence.

Instead, try perceiving your skills as dynamic. This mindset can help transform the "I am lousy at this so I will never be able to do it" thoughts, into "I need to work on this so that I can do better next time!" thoughts. Remember, practice makes perfect – or perhaps I should say practice makes for excellence! We aren't all born with the ability to solve complex math problems, but we do have the ability to learn, acquire new skills and further develop them. If you find that you aren't seeing the results you would like, try taking a different approach to your studies. One of my favorite sayings is 'when things don't go right, go left.'

Just in case you feel that you have exhausted every option in attempting to improve in a particular subject, I thought I should let you in on a little secret. When I first started studying my undergraduate degree in psychology, the thought of a compulsory statistics unit every year was not something that had crossed my mind! I actually felt a sense of relief thinking that psychology couldn't possibly place an emphasis on knowing how to conduct statistical analyses! I found the classes challenging, and although I passed my assignments, I didn't do as well as I had hoped. It was only as the years progressed that I finally understood – and dare I say enjoyed – learning statistics! I went from dreading the subject at the beginning of my degree, to being one of the top students in the class and finishing in the top 5% of my course! It really is amazing what determination, perseverance and a change in mindset can do!

My Top 5 Tips
For Dealing With Disappointment

 Aim for excellence, not perfection.

 Read over your teacher's feedback carefully and identify what you did wrong as well as what you did right!

 Make a time to meet with your teacher to discuss your assignment and the feedback.

 Remember that your skills are dynamic and that you can improve in them!

 Try taking a different approach to your studies and using other methods to help you understand the topic.

Staying Up to Date

When I was in my final years of high school, I would spend the majority of my lunch breaks and free lessons hidden away in one of the soundproof silent rooms in my school library. Actually, contrary to the teachers' knowledge, there was only ever really one silent room. The other somehow became infamous for being more of a 'fun zone' to a group of boys in my year. Most of the time, they would go into the room, close the door behind them, and have screaming competitions with each other. It was really quite amusing to peep through the glass window, seeing them all running amok, screaming at the top of their lungs whilst barely being able to hear them! Come to think of it, perhaps not everyone in my year level used his or her time as wisely as I did? Don't worry, I most certainly wasn't the only one playing social hibernation throughout the school day! Most of my friends would also join me halfway through lunchtime or in between classes to fit in an extra study session and catch up on homework. Somehow we managed not to allow ourselves to get distracted by all of the boys' antics as they walked in and out of the room next door!

I found it extremely helpful to use these gaps in the day to work on my assignments and in particular, to review my class notes. My new little study routine originally began as a way to juggle school and dance, freeing up some necessary time in the evenings so that I could still make it to my classes in the city. Even so, I continued on with my routine all the way through to my final year at university. Fortunately, most of my lectures were not scheduled back-to-back, so I was able to use my breaks in between classes to work on my weekly summaries. I would take my laptop and textbooks up to the top floor of the library, spread my books out in one of the study cubicles and get working. My notes were usually in dire need of a polish after class! This was mainly due to my tendency to try and get down as much information as I possibly could incase I would ever miss out on a crucial piece of information that slipped out of my lecturers' lips. I would usually spend a good twenty minutes skimming over my work, fixing up headings and highlighting the key points. On top of that, I would typically pick up on a few points that, when I looked over them after class, somehow didn't seem to make sense anymore. These notes would then be written down on a separate notepad titled: "QUESTIONS TO ADDRESS" and I would set aside some time to come back and review them. If I didn't happen to have much luck on my own, then the chances were that my lecturer was soon about to receive one of my all-too-familiar emails in the desperate hope that they would be available later that week to clarify my questions and put my mind at ease. Either way, by setting aside some time each day to review my notes, I was able to stay on top of my work and come exam time, feel much more prepared!

Writing Weekly Summaries

Writing weekly summaries is the most effective way to stay on top of your class work throughout the busy school year. Doing so will help you consolidate your learning throughout the semester and also identify any areas that might need further clarifying. Apart from helping you avoid last minute cramming, another reason why I am particularly fond of writing weekly summaries is because they make for an excellent resource come exam time. Instead of having to read through all of your class notes and densely packed information textbooks, your summaries are able to act as your own compact study guide, making for a much more time-efficient resource for studying for your exams!

While I don't expect for you to fill up your free periods and lunchtimes with more studying, I highly recommend that you try to review your notes and keep adding to your weekly summaries as often as you can. Did you know that the vast majority of information that we are likely to forget occurs within the first twenty-four hours of learning something new? By regularly setting aside time to write your weekly summaries, you will be able to retain a significantly larger amount of information than otherwise possible. In turn, this makes studying for exams a lot easier and far more efficient! I took great pride in writing my summaries, to the point that as the end of the semester drew nearer and I had finished summarising the final weeks' content, I would look forward to having my notes bound - not to mention choosing a custom front and back cover! Then again, being the organization lover that I am, would you have expected anything less? Once the exams were over I would store my booklets in the hallway closet. In fact, I still have all of them from my final year at university carefully lined up on the top shelf, just in case I ever need to refer back to them. Besides, I never know when I might want to flip through them and arm myself with some more fun facts!

Structuring Your Summaries

There's no one rule you must abide by when structuring your weekly summaries, however I do have a few very useful suggestions to help you transform your lengthy notes into a practical revision tool.

 Keep It Short

First off, it's important to remember that your weekly summaries are just that – summaries. Make sure to keep them brief, restricting them to no more than four to five pages per week. Otherwise, you might end up with your very own limited edition, one of a kind textbook that is just as densely packed as the one you purchased at the start of the year! One way to keep your summaries concise is to keep in mind the subtopics you learned in class each week. This will help stop you from veering off track and including unnecessary information, which is unlikely to feature in future class tests and exams. If you like, consider writing the subtopics at the top of the page before starting on your summaries, to ensure you stick to the relevant content and only include key information. While not essential, it can also be a good idea to use dot points rather than writing out lengthy statements and descriptions. Often, I would write out definitions and quotes in full and restrict the rest of my notes to dot points in order to minimize the length of my summaries. After all, you want to be able to condense both your class notes and notes from any additional readings and handouts, so it's important that you make sure you are being concise!

 Use Visual Aids

Apart from keeping your summaries brief, it is also important that the information clearly stands out. Let's face it; even though your summaries are able to drastically condense your notes, you may not always have the time or energy to read through several weeks' worth of summaries. While the aim is for them to be a practical study tool, when you happen to find yourself in a busy week and consumed with responsibilities and unexpected homework, it all comes down to convenience. You want reviewing your summaries to require minimal effort on your behalf. I'm not saying that you should be able to mindlessly read over your notes, but rather that the information is eye catching and practically pops out in front of you at a glance so that you cannot help but notice what is written! Using color to annotate your notes will enable key words to stand out. Just like you would highlight or underline important words in an essay question, make sure you do the same in your summaries. You might also like to color code your notes, highlighting subtopics, questions, definitions and examples all in different colors. Visual cues are highly effective and I am always recommending they be put to good use wherever possible! Whenever I would write my summaries, I would find it helpful to also include illustrations and diagrams. I found this technique was most useful when trying to simplify complex information or make a particular theory or concept more meaningful.

My Top 5 Tips
For Writing Weekly Summaries

 Write your weekly summaries while the information you have learned is fresh in your mind.

 Keep your summaries short and concise by writing down only the main ideas and important details.

 Make sure you include information from your class notes and additional readings and handouts.

 Include visual aids such as diagrams and charts to simplify complex information.

 Rely on your weekly summaries to help you study for exams!

Studying For Finals

I was always under the impression that the harder I worked, the better I would do in school. It's pretty obvious isn't it? The more you study, the more familiar with the material you will become and the more likely you are to get a good grade. Right? Wrong! While hard work is definitely a key ingredient for being successful in any area of life, it most certainly is not the only factor. How you study is just as important, if not more! I sure wish I knew this back when I was tallying up the total number of hours I planned on studying for my exams, thinking that I had found the key to success! I remember one evening sitting in my room with one of my final drafts of an English essay that I had written in preparation for my end of year exam. I had written out each paragraph five times over and then tested myself to see if I could re-write the entire paper word-for-word under timed conditions. It took me three hours and thirty sheets of paper but several hand cramps later, I had finally mastered my essay. Unfortunately, there was a range of possible essay questions that the examiners could have asked in the exam, which meant I had to repeat this pursuit multiple times over. What else was I supposed to do? We are always told to study for exams and assignments but I can't remember a time when I was instructed on how to study! When it came to learning new words, recalling definitions, understanding theories or remembering essays, this seemed like the best option at the time.

One afternoon, when I was studying at university, I met with a friend to prepare for one of our major exams that were coming up at the end of the semester. We ended up finding an unoccupied room in one of the old psychology buildings and turning it into our little study cave for the next few weeks. When we put our bags down, I suggested we'd better get started so that we can make the most of the day and try to cover as much of the material as possible. Contrary to my typical study habits, she surprised me and said that she never studied that way. She preferred to choose a couple of subtopics and focus on those. Whether it was going to take up the entire afternoon or not did not concern her. At first I didn't want to seem pushy and thought I could always fit in some extra time to review the material later that night, however that never happened... I realized that I got a lot more out of my study sessions by breaking up the course content and giving a few subtopics my undivided attention each day. On top of that, we made our regular study sessions fun, goofing around and making up silly word associations and acronyms, as well as attempting to draw cartoons and illustrations on the whiteboard. Our creativity even led us to design a giant colorful poster that outlined every assessment and psychological test we had learned that semester – and trust me, there were a lot!

Preparing For Finals

Before you begin studying for your exams, make sure to write down your exam dates in a calendar. While some might say it's enough to simply write these important dates down in your school diary or planner, having your exam dates written in a calendar and displaying it in your room will help to create a sense of urgency and motivate you to get studying! Given my love for bunnies and all things fluffy, you can probably picture exactly what my wall calendar looks like! Baby bunnies one year and baby bunnies and puppies the next! Oh and of course, I can't forget last year's calendar - baby bunnies and their lookalike kittens! In my defense, when I was in my second year of studying an undergraduate diploma of psychology, my lecturer told us that looking at pictures of baby animals stimulates a certain area of the brain that assists with enhancing brain performance during academic tasks, like an exam. Evidently, I was a very dedicated student and had calculated every possible way to potentially boost my final grade!

Apart from the oh-so-cute photos of furry baby animals and big red asterisks to represent my exams, there was something else that was always displayed on my calendar. I used to write down the topics for each of my subjects that I needed to revise and space these out across all of the days. I highly recommend creating a study timeline and selecting several topics that you plan to revise each day. This will help you to effectively spread out your revision over the weeks leading up to the exam and assist you in dividing your time between each subject. Most importantly, planning your approach in advance will bring some much-needed structure into your study sessions. Also, you can be sure that as long as you do your best to stick to your study calendar, you can feel confident walking into your exam venue knowing you are well prepared!

To make sure that you cover all of the necessary topics, it can be useful to first make a separate study checklist. Be sure to not only write down the main topics you studied in class, but also the subtopics that will need to be revised. Just remember that not every topic will require the same amount of time, so try and take this into account when creating your study timeline.

Example of my study checklist:

subject 1	subject 2

Topic A

  Subtopic 1
  Subtopic 2
  Subtopic 3

Topic B

  Subtopic 1
  Subtopic 2
  Subtopic 3

subject 3	subject 4

Study Smart Not Hard

If you take one thing from this chapter, it should be that repeatedly reading over your notes and re-writing information is not your only option when revising for exams. It is however one of the most common study strategies used by students. Of course, this study method has its place in your overall study routine, however you won't see me wearing its team colors any time soon. The reason why this strategy is not my favorite is because it often involves passive learning, making it ineffective and tedious when it comes time to consolidate those large amounts of information into your long-term memory. If I had to make a comparison, I would say it's a lot like having a conversation in a café and then expecting the person sitting on the table next to you to have known exactly what you were talking about. Unless they were eavesdropping, it's highly likely that they weren't paying attention because your conversation was not meaningful to them. If you want to learn something, you need to make it meaningful and actively pay attention!

The best kinds of study techniques are therefore those that require active learning. Active learning requires you to make numerous connections between the information so that your mind can begin to process it effectively. Activities such as drawing mind maps and having class discussions or debates all help to promote analysis, synthesis and evaluation of the information that you are trying to learn. Whilst these techniques often require more effort on your end, the upside is that they are far more effective, meaning you won't need to spend as much time revising the information later on!

The Four Learning Styles

There are numerous study techniques that you can implement into your exam revision sessions. Given the scope, sometimes it is a matter of trial and error in order to see which suits you best. Each study technique is tailored to one of the four learning styles: Visual, Auditory, Read and Write, and Kinesthetic. This does not mean that each of us should be relying solely on one particular group of techniques, though this is a commonly held misconception! It is important to consider which methods will likely work best for you, however each study technique has something unique to offer and may come in handy when learning a particular topic. Many people also find that adding some variety into their study sessions and mixing things up helps to keep their study sessions fresh. No one likes boring or repetitive study sessions!

While I do have a tendency to gravitate towards techniques that heavily rely on visual cues, I would never discount the benefits of a group discussion or a catchy song to help me study. Thinking back to my exam study sessions, I would to rely on a range of different techniques, depending on the topic I was studying. Sometimes, you could have found me rolling out large sheets of cardboard and creating detailed mind maps when studying different theories. Other times, I was quizzing myself with flashcards or relying on acronyms to help me remember several small pieces of information. I was even stubborn enough to coax my sister into listening to me recite my lists of definitions and then have her quiz me on all the answers I got incorrect. What's more, I used to – and still do - act out my presentations using interpretive dance to help me remember the main ideas. Perhaps you think I am stretching the truth, however I assure you, there have been times when my family has walked in on me rehearsing my presentation with my hands up in the air trying to make them into a shape that only made sense to me!

Here are some different study techniques you might like to try that are tailored to each of the four types of learning styles.

Visual Techniques

- Create mind maps.
- Color-co-ordinate your notes.
- Quiz yourself using flash cards.
- Draw diagrams and charts.
- Watch a short clip or movie about your topic.
- Turn sentences into pictures.

Auditory Techniques

- Try recording your notes and playing them back.
- Host a group study session.
- Get involved in class discussions.
- Try reading the material out loud.
- Make up rhymes or songs about key theories and concepts.
- Use word association

Kinesthetic Techniques

- Build a 3D model or diagram.
- Go on a field trip where possible.
- Act out the information.
- Include a physical activity while you study.

Read and Write Techniques

- Re-write your notes as a revision exercise.
- Turn diagrams and charts into words.
- Ask your lecturer or teacher for handouts.
- Read from multiple resources such as the Internet, textbooks and articles.
- Write a creative piece about the information you are learning.
- Take detailed notes in class.

My Top 5 Tips
For Studying For Exams

 Write your exam dates in a calendar and display it in your room.

 Create a study checklist to ensure you cover the necessary material.

 Limit your study sessions to several topics per day.

 Make sure to engage in active learning and make the information meaningful to you.

 Trial a range of study techniques to discover which are most effective for you.

How to Throw The Ultimate Study Party!

You didn't really think I would forget to talk about my favorite thing of all, did you? When I started my YouTube channel in early 2015 I was determined to make studying fun – or at least as fun as possible! I wanted to take the stress out of having to prepare for exams and bring an element of lightheartedness to the typical study sessions that take place each day. I remember my group study sessions always being extremely helpful, however I wanted to spice things up. There I was, daring to be different and showing no shame, wearing a party hat, throwing some confetti in front of the camera and answering all of your study questions while indulging in my favorite treat – marshmallows! I was ready and willing to put myself out there and in doing so, had a lot of fun! Even if it was just me sitting alone in my room talking to a camera and laughing at myself in the reflection of the lens, I knew that in time there would be thousands of faces watching attentively on their phones and laptops. Picturing a few friendly faces certainly helped me feel less alone at the very start, too! To think that my YouTube channel has had such a huge impact on so many students' study sessions and the way they view their studies overall, was something I couldn't and still can't entirely comprehend. One thing I do know is that being able to bring a smile to someone's face is exactly what drives me to continually keep innovating and coming up with new ways to make your time at school as enjoyable and as positive of an experience as possible!

Banishing Boring Study Sessions

I mentioned earlier that one of the most important ingredients for academic success is your attitude and overall approach to studying. We spend so much time studying that it's vital we find enjoyment in what we are learning. After all, if you enjoy what you are learning and keep a positive mindset, then the benefits will noticeably shine through in your grades. Imagine sitting down to study and actually feeling excited? That with every skill you acquired, every topic you conquered and every assignment you completed, you felt confident and were actually enjoying yourself? I know, it sounds completely farfetched, doesn't it? Well, if you ask me, it's time to take a stand and make some necessary changes to the once-dreaded study sessions. It's time to shake things up, throw some confetti and banish those boring study sessions once and for all! Besides, who said throwing a party should be reserved for birthdays and special occasions? I certainly disagree! Whether you are looking for a way to boost your motivation or need to reignite that spark which fuels your passion for learning, this is the perfect, easy and fun solution to your problems. So get out your phones and send a text to your closest study buddies, create a Facebook event or hand out custom invites because it's study party time!

Study Party Essentials

There are a few must-haves when it comes to throwing the ultimate study party. Of course, the success of your study party is not determined by how many streamers you have

PARTY TIME!

I'M HAVING A PARTY!

FOR:

DATE: next Sunday

PLACE: my house

TIME: 2-4 pm

RSVP: end of the week

make sure you bring your notes, some yummy snacks and positive vibes!

See you then!
xo Jess

or whether you and your friends have brought enough chocolate and sweets to share. While these things can help to get you into party mode, my list of essentials consists of a few other important factors to make your study parties both fun and productive! Here is what you will need:

- Your best study buddies
- A distraction-free study zone
- Your favorite party snacks
- Party decorations (streamers, party hats, balloons, confetti etc.)
- Your textbooks and class notes
- Pens, highlighters, markers and paper
- Positive vibes!

Game Time!

Now that you are all set up and your friends have arrived, it's time to get your study on! Being a study party, you want to make sure that you are revising and reviewing your notes in a way that makes studying fun. I mean, you can't go to all the effort of throwing a party, only to have your group of friends sit in a circle, reciting their notes to each other! Besides, this boring study technique is usually why group study sessions can end up unproductive, and go from being focused on preparing for exams one minute, to crowding around a laptop and watching cat videos on YouTube the next! Instead, if you and your friends are in the early stages of reviewing the material, try relying on more interactive forms of studying. Drawing colorful mind maps on large sheets of paper, writing your notes on a white board, or creating tables to contrast between different concepts are all great ways of revising that ensure everyone is included and has a hands-on approach to studying.

Once you all have a grasp on the topics, it's time for some party games! I like to put my own personal spin on some typical party games and use them as a way to make a group study session loads of fun! Here are a few different games you might like to play, to help your friends get into study party mode:

1. Pictionary

Begin by dividing your group of study buddies into pairs. Next, write down a list of concepts, definitions or theories on some cut up pieces of paper before folding them in half and placing them in a hat or bowl. Each pair should take turns to draw from the hat or bowl and attempt to act out their piece of paper to the group. If the partner guesses correctly before the rest of the group, then that pair is awarded one point. The pair with the most number of correct answers at the end of each round is the winning pair!

2. The Chocolate Game

This game is my personal favorite! Simply place a block of chocolate in the middle of the circle with a plastic fork and knife. Have each person write down at least five questions on different pieces of paper and place them in a bowl in the middle of the circle. Take turns picking a question to answer. Once a question is answered correctly, the person can use the knife and fork to cut the chocolate and eat as much as they can, until the next person answers a question correctly. You have to act fast if you want to get the chocolate!

3. Buzz Time Trivia

Nominate one of your friends to be the 'quizmaster' and assemble the rest of your friends into two groups who will battle it out to win! The quizmaster will be in charge of creating a deck of flash cards and will read out one question at a time. Whichever group buzzes in to answer the question correctly first is given one point. The winning group is then determined once the entire deck of flash cards has been read.

While these are my favorite party games to play, there are many others that you and your friends can opt for. In fact, if you happen to feel like being even more creative, you might like to invent your own games too! Ultimately, it's all about making your group study sessions as interactive and enjoyable as possible so that you all get the most out of your revision time. So next time you reach for your textbook, remember to also reach for your party hat and invite your friends over for a study party!

My Top 5 Tips
For Throwing A Study Party

 Use the beginning of your study party to briefly review the material, before studying each topic more in depth.

 Opt for interactive forms of studying, rather than re-reading your notes to each other.

 Invite only your closest study buddies whom you work well with.

 Make sure everyone contributes by bringing something to the party such as food, drinks, decorations or games.

 Play games to make your study party fun and engaging!

Overcoming Study Stress and Anxiety

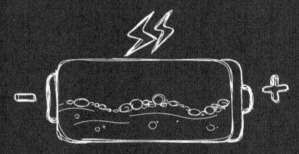

While I certainly did a good job of hiding it in the past, when I was younger I was no stranger to feeling stressed and overwhelmed. This was especially the case when things would begin to heat up at school, such as during exam time! It didn't take long for my extended hours of studying and lack of personal 'me time' to leave me feeling emotionally vulnerable and physically run down. What most people recognize and describe as a kaleidoscope of butterflies, was usually what I referred to as a heard of elephants, stomping around at the pit of my stomach. Needless to say, their regular visits drained me of my energy and left my parents feeling concerned as they watched on in the hope that I would not self-destruct like the many students that had before me.

At first, feeling anxious was something that evoked a sense of fear within me. I was scared it was out of my control and I was unaware how to manage the waves of emotion that washed over me and knocked me about. I hadn't quite learned to take responsibility for my own actions and their subsequent consequences. Eventually, I drew the connection between the demands and expectations I was placing on myself and I soon began to learn how to take control of my life and manage my anxiety. I wish I could say that all it took was a quick pep talk or an unexpected light bulb moment, however the truth is that it took far more discipline on my end than that. I realized that I needed to be kind to myself; to allow myself some time off from studying, to practice living a well-balanced life and to focus on attending to all areas of my life, rather than neglecting all but one.

Only recently however did I really take a step back and realize just how far I have come in a short time. It was late last year that I was speaking to one of my friends on the phone when she asked me how my anxiety was going. "What do you mean?" I asked, as though I had forgotten all about it! Then it hit me. Those all too familiar elephants had not paid me a visit in over six months. It was not because they had forgotten about me, but rather because I had made some necessary changes to my life that did not warrant their frequent visits anymore. Of course, I still get nervous from time-to-time and I still know what it feels like to be overwhelmed by an increasing workload, but I also know that there are many ways for me to help myself whenever I notice those elephants in the distance.

Feeling Stressed!

Everyone experiences feeling stressed or anxious from time-to-time. While we all respond to specific situations differently, there are a few circumstances in particular that likely elicit a stress response. Have you ever tried to get a good night's sleep when you know you have a pile of homework waiting impatiently for you on your desk? Perhaps you've experienced the racing thoughts that are often accompanied by a knot it your stomach the night before an important exam? Maybe it's just been a particularly busy month and the ongoing demands of your homework and assignments collectively leave you tensing your muscles and driving your shoulders all the way up to greet your ears? However you respond to stressful situations, know that you are not alone. Remember that feeling stressed, nervous, anxious or overwhelmed when things become a little too much to handle is completely normal! The important thing is to be able to identify how you are feeling so that you can be proactive. After all, the way you feel is your body's way of letting you know that something needs to change with regards to your current situation. Perhaps it's your perception of your studies, your overall workload, the demands and expectations you place on yourself, or your environment, such as the friends you surround yourself with? For me, it was about finding balance between my studies and personal life, as well as removing unrealistic expectations that I placed on myself when it came to my grades.

How To Avoid Study Burnout

Feeling stressed for a prolonged amount of time can ultimately cause you to feel tired and run down. In an attempt to avoid feeling burnt out – especially during the school year – it's important that you find balance and learn to make time for both your studies and other commitments. While it can be easy to cast all other responsibilities and your social life aside when a major assignment or exam nears closer, it's important that you still make time for them. After all, no matter how important it is, there is more to life than school. In fact, attending to other areas of your life will allow you to be your best, energized and most happy self, so that you can continue to focus in class, complete and take pride in your assignments, and overall, excel in school!

Self Care

With each year that you advance in your studies, comes an increasingly challenging and demanding workload. Since there is no way of convincing your teachers to cancel homework (despite the failed efforts of many of my old classmates!), it's up to you to actively set aside time to focus on your personal needs. There will always be something that tries to grab your attention and trust me; these responsibilities and demands have a way of lingering throughout your adult life. There will always be just one more page to read, one more question to answer, or one more email to send... The trick is not to let it take priority over what matters most - you!

Try and avoid retreating into a little study cave, only to reappear once your workload resumes back to normal. When I was in my final years of high school, I remember entering into what could only be considered 'study hibernation.' My cave was the library and I had no intention of leaving! Unlike a bear however, that is ready to re-enter the world after its extended sleep cycle, by the time my exams were over, I felt as though I needed to go into hibernation for real! I strongly advise that you don't follow suit, waiting until after things quiet down to justify being able to set aside some important 'me time.' Doing something for yourself can be as simple as scheduling in time in your planner to go for a walk, watch a movie, go out for dinner, or take a relaxing bath. However you like to treat yourself for all of your hard work, do it.

Exercise

One of the best forms of self-care is exercise! Unfortunately, this is also one that most often gets pushed to the bottom of the to-do list and gets postponed until a free time slot opens up. The truth is, you don't need to sweat out a one-hour gym session, play a full game of soccer or take a dance class in order to get some exercise. Getting outdoors for even fifteen minutes a day brings numerous health benefits. Go for a walk in your local park, get out your jump rope, or go for a short bike ride around your neighborhood. All of these are going to get your heart rate up, leaving you feeling more alert, energized and most importantly, less stressed! This is because when you exercise, your body releases endorphins that help to combat feelings of stress and also help to promote a good night's sleep - something you definitely can't do without when you have to stay focused all day long in class.

 Seek Support

While all of these strategies can collectively help you to manage your stress levels throughout the year, I know that for some, feeling stressed or anxious can be an ongoing challenge. It may not be something that you experience for years on end, or even months at a time, however if you find that you are struggling to carry the weight of your responsibilities, I highly recommend talking to someone. Seeking support from a family member, friend or even staff member can remind you that you are not alone. Often, simply talking about your situation can already begin to take some of the pressure off. Remember, there is always someone there to help and offer you advice and guidance.

I always found it helpful to talk to my mother when I was having a tough time at school. Even though she couldn't complete my assignments for me or be present during an exam to slip me the correct answer, being able to express how I was feeling was always a big help! Sometimes, I just needed some reassurance, while other times, talking about my situation helped me to realize what I needed to do for myself in order to feel better.

My Top **5** Tips
For Managing Stress

 Don't hide your feelings. Acknowledge when you feel stressed or anxious.

 Be proactive and try implementing different strategies to help you feel calmer.

 Establish a healthy work-life balance and remember not to neglect your hobbies and social commitments.

 Engage in regular self-care to avoid experiencing study burn out.

 Seek support and talk about your situation with a family member, teacher or friend.

Surviving Exam Week

When I was in high school, I had to take my final exams with my entire year of one hundred and twenty classmates in a huge, echoing hall. My first exam was for my English class and I remember waiting impatiently outside the glass double doors with my friends to enter the exam venue. We tried to catch a glimpse from the outside, despite having zero chance of actually being able to see what was on the exam paper! Once inside, we made our way to our assigned seating. As luck would have it, there I was; seated front row center under the watchful eyes of the examiner. I distinctly recall feeling a wave of panic rush over me at that point. All I could picture in that moment was the large clock hanging on the wall at the front of the room and a big black garbage bin located right at the front, only two, maybe three feet away. Those panicky feelings suddenly transformed into anxious thoughts as I began to contemplate my worse case scenario. Was I going to be that student who gets sick in front of the entire year?

Those first ten minutes of reading time could not have gone any slower! I began to glance over the exam questions, feeling somewhat lightheaded. But then, page-by-page, I slowly noticed my anxieties subsiding. The tension and panic that had started to swell inside my chest had all of a sudden washed away and I could feel the blood rush back to my face. Although I was still full of adrenaline, it wasn't leaving me feeling helpless. I felt my body enter into 'fight mode' and I was ready and eager to tackle those exam questions. "I've got this!" I said to myself with a smile. I knew exactly what I had to do and how to answer the questions - nothing was a surprise to me. I had been preparing for this exam for months and it was time for all of my hard work to finally pay off. I snatched up my pen from the desk, charged at the paper, and for those few hours, my mind was fixated on the pages in front of me. Somehow, all of the information that I had stored away in my brain over the year began spilling out. My mind was an open textbook and it was as if I could hear my English teacher coaching me through the whole exam.

As I wrote my final sentence and finally came up for air, I looked back at the clock that was hanging above the space where the examiner had been standing at the start. I could not believe it: I had finished the exam with forty-five minutes to spare! Surely I mustn't have been the only one? I looked around to see a sea of heads hunched over their desks and realized everyone else was still writing. I then used the remaining time to review my work and make some necessary touch-ups. Upon leaving the exam, I felt confident - well that and a great sense of relief! I realized that I really should have given myself more credit. I guess it's easy to lose sight of our own abilities and lack confidence when put under pressure to perform.

What To Do The Week Of Exams

You've spent weeks revising for your upcoming exams and now that they are only a week away, there are a few important things to remember and do to help you perform at your best! It's usually at this point that many students get into a bit of a 'study frenzy,' spending the majority of their time locked away in a library with their heads buried in their text books. Unless you have forgotten about your exams and failed to begin your revision with enough time to spare, there is no reason why this week should be overly stressful. Remember, by now you would have gone over your class notes and readings, as well as familiarized yourself with the main concepts, theories and facts – not to mention you have been reviewing your notes and writing your weekly summaries since the beginning of the semester, right? As you have prepared yourself throughout the whole year, instead of trying to cram or panic about what is on the exam, you are able to use this time wisely. Go over your notes and take this as an opportunity to review them in more detail, picking up on all of those points that teachers love to include in exams to differentiate between students who have studied well and those who have studied exceptionally well and know the subject inside out! Once you think you have thoroughly covered everything, try and access some practice papers and test yourself under exam conditions. Completing past papers and practice tests is the best way to assess your understanding of the subject and identify any unexpected gaps in your knowledge. Also, practicing under exam conditions and recreating a similar environment can help make this whole process less daunting!

My Top 5 Tips For Completing Exams:

1 Cover all potential answers when reading a multiple-choice question. Brainstorm what you know about the topic first, before looking at the potential answers to avoid getting confused.

2 Gain extra time on an exam by using reading time to answer multiple-choice questions. On average, you will solve one question per minute. That means you could answer up to 10 multiple-choice questions in the first minute of writing time!

3 Make sure to adapt previously learned essays to the essay question to avoid losing marks and responding to the question incorrectly.

4 Make sure to show your workings. If you answer a question incorrectly but your workings were still correct, then you can still earn some marks!

5 Always turn your exam booklet over. You'd be surprised how many students forget to answer questions that were written on the back!

Dealing With Exam Anxiety

While I have already shared my top tips for managing stress and anxiety throughout the year, managing exam anxiety can be slightly different. I thought I should also mention a few of my go-to strategies for dealing with those uncomfortable moments that sometimes arise during exams...

 Be Confident

Often, it is the pressure we place on ourselves to get a certain grade that can contribute to our levels of stress and anxiety. On top of this, negative thought patterns and those detrimental 'what if?' questions could lead you to doubt in your abilities. While completing an exam can seem daunting, as long as you have studied effectively, there should not be anything new or too difficult for you to get caught up over. Believe it or not, your teachers and your school want you to succeed and it's in their best interests that you do! Instead of worrying about everything that could go wrong, use your exam as an opportunity for you to demonstrate your knowledge. Show your teachers and prove to yourself just how much you have learned. Remain confident in your abilities to tackle this next exam and remember that you have survived exams before, so there is no reason why you won't get through this one, too! Even if you do come across a question that you are unsure of how to answer, tell yourself that it's okay and consider revisiting it later if you have some extra time. There is no use dwelling on a question. Usually, allowing yourself to come back to it will help you to approach it differently and come up with the answer.

 Be Comfortable

When I was in high school we had to wear our school uniforms for our exams, although once I got to university, the freedom to choose what I wore each day was something I never took for granted! If you have the option to wear whatever you like to your exams, make sure you dress comfortably. Now, please don't think that showing up in your pajamas is something I am condoning! Just be practical when choosing your outfit. Perhaps it's best to avoid the tight waistband of your skinny jeans or itchy fabric of a woolen sweater that could leave you sitting in your chair feeling restricted? Apart from dressing appropriately, I would always bring a few of my exam essentials into the venue with me. Consider bringing a bottle of water, a packet of tissues and a small snack, such as a muesli bar into your exam. Let's face it; sitting in a hall for up to three hours or more isn't a normal day for most of us, so you want to have all of the necessary essentials with you to help you settle in!

 Go Step-By-Step

It doesn't matter how many questions your exam booklet contains. Whether you are required to write three essays or answer one hundred and twenty multiple-choice questions, there is only ever one thing that you can do to make your exam seem less overwhelming - focus on one question at a time! I always recommend skimming through the exam questions during reading time to familiarize yourself with the whole paper, however when reading time concludes, it's best to give each question your undivided attention. Besides, remember 'how you eat that elephant?' Precisely! 'One bite at a time!' Think of your exam paper as that big elephant. No matter the size, when you focus on each task individually, it all becomes a lot more manageable!

Breathe

Deep breathing is an excellent and extremely simple way to feel calm and manage stress and anxiety. Try taking a few deep breaths before you begin your exam as well as whenever you start to feel nervous. I always recommend slowing down your breathing by inhaling to the count of four and exhaling to the count of six. When you lengthen your exhalations to be longer than your inhalations, your body begins to switch on your parasympathetic nervous system, which will calm you down. Also, focusing on something as simple as breathing helps to quieten those racing thoughts by acting as a temporary and soothing distraction!

My Top 5 Tips
For Surviving Exam Week

 Make sure you have revised every topic listed on your exam checklist.

 Do practice tests to assess your knowledge and get used to answering questions under exam conditions.

 View your exams as an opportunity for you to demonstrate your knowledge.

 Be confident in your abilities and know that you have survived exams before.

 Enter the exam with a plan of attack and remember to always do your best!

The Next Step...

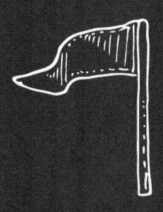

For many, deciding what career pathway to choose and what degree to study after high school can be challenging. It's not always clear-cut and clarity doesn't always grace everyone during the final years of high school. I remember thinking to myself how lucky I was to know exactly what I wanted to do after I graduated high school. I had a clear action plan. I was going to study psychology and follow in my older sister's footsteps by joining the sea of students at Monash University. After all, it was considered to be one of the top universities in the state. In hindsight, I realize just how naive I was at the time. I thought I had my future all figured out - like it could be that simple. I pictured my life ten years down the track and was certain of what my future had in store for me. After high school, I worked hard for the next five years and devoted myself to my studies while simultaneously holding four volunteer jobs over the course of my undergraduate and postgraduate degrees. I loved everything about university life; the passionate lecturers, the interesting subjects, the dedicated tutors, and my newly formed friendships. I thrived in my environment and loved that I was constantly being challenged academically, whilst also growing emotionally. To top it off, I saw all of my hard work finally pay off and I graduated from university with honors.

Late one night however, while I was on holidays, I suddenly sat up in bed, and it was as if in that moment, my whole life-plan dramatically shifted. I was overcome by a wave of excitement - I had an idea for a new and exciting venture. Like a pebble being dropped into a pond that creates a cascading effect on the water's surface, it was this moment that would change the course of my life and bring with it exciting new opportunities. I began sketching a line of educational stationery for students, which turned into what is now my stationery line seed.ED Educationery. Shortly after I began creating the initial sketches, I was overcome by not only the desire, but by a need to begin creating educational YouTube videos to help students around the world. I wanted to make studying easier and more accessible. I wanted to be a positive role model for young people and I had a burning desire and passion to do so.

At first, the idea of starting my own business, making videos on YouTube and entering into the realm of education unsettled, if not overwhelmed me. I had spent so many years dedicating myself to the mental health sector and couldn't justify throwing it all away. I was torn between an old and a newfound passion. "How can I throw away five years of studying psychology?" This thought raced through my mind for a week as I sat with the idea of leaving behind a large part of myself. Then it hit me; it wasn't all for nothing. Everything I had learned - all of the skills gained throughout my time at school and university - they were transferable and would serve me in some way. If it weren't for my education, I would never have become the self-motivated and conscientious person I am today. If it weren't for the volunteer work that I completed to complement my studies, I would never have learned the value of empathy, non-judgment, understanding and other valuable communication skills. I certainly would never have developed my time-management and organizational skills without being put under pressure to work towards a deadline and complete all of my assignments. Importantly, I would never have developed my writing skills without having to complete all of those essays along with that twenty-five thousand-word thesis at the end of my degree. All of these skills have helped me to run my own business, to create informative content on my channel, to interact with my fans and to even write this book. It didn't matter that I had decided to change career paths. What mattered was that I had the tools and was equipped to do so, because of my education. It was my education that opened doors to numerous possibilities and gave me the opportunity to create the life I once dreamed of – even if the path wasn't as I had originally expected!

Deciding A Career Pathway

When it comes to deciding what degree to study and what career pathway to choose, first thing's first; don't discount any options that even remotely spark your interest. Keep an open mind and try to brainstorm a whole range of careers, before narrowing down your choices and selecting your top few. Don't just settle for the first few jobs that come to mind. Besides, we all know the popular careers available to us - doctor, lawyer, teacher, nurse etc. Apart from these, there are so many other degrees and jobs available that never existed before. I never could have imagined being a YouTuber when I was younger - it didn't even exist! If you are still having trouble coming up with a list of professions that you feel you could be suited to, consider talking to your school guidance counsellor or careers counsellor. Often, they will have some great advice and can help you decide what you should do once you graduate from school.

Once you have narrowed down your choices, it's important that you do your research. Don't be shy to ask older students about their experience at university or speak to someone in a profession of interest to see how they enjoy what they do for a living. It's always helpful to hear it first hand from someone else. Plus, if you have any questions then these are the best people to ask! Apart from talking to others and seeking out their advice, internships and work experience are great ways to acquire some real-life experience, which can help you decide whether a particular career is right for you! Understanding what it's like to be in a certain profession can give you clarity and affirm whether this career pathway is something you want to do in the future.

The following questions are here to help get you thinking about potential careers that you would best be suited to. You might find clear patterns in your answers that are screaming out at you, telling you exactly how you should be spending your time. At the very least, you will be able to pick up on some common themes, such as creativity, education, caring for others, or being physically active.

Choosing The Right University For You!

There is a common misconception that top ranking universities should always be given first preference when deciding which course to study. Every study institution is known for its own area(s) of strength, so it's important that you research each one and make sure that your field of study is known for being one of its strong-points. This is crucial because there may be another university or study institution with better facilities, as well as more employment opportunities for you once you graduate! To get a better feel for the places that interest you, consider attending a university fair, or better yet, an open day. This is a great opportunity for you to speak with faculty members

P op Quiz!

1 The most important thing in life is:
- -

2 I value those who:
- -

3 I would like to do more of:
- -

4 I am most skilled at:
- -

5 I want to be known for:
- -

6 My favorite subject is:
- -

7 In my spare time I enjoy doing:
- -

8 I would love to know more about:
- -

9 My strongest subject is:
- -

10 I am passionate about :
- -

and students and find out more about various programs and opportunities that the universities offer, helping you decide which one would be a good fit for you! Bear in mind that when deciding which university to attend, it's important that the courses spark your interest and that you also feel comfortable in your surroundings. You want to make sure that the atmosphere, student life, and university culture all suit you. After all, you are going to be enrolled to study there for several years and want to enjoy your entire experience!

Considering A Gap Year

While this is not something that is usually discussed in your high school classroom, deciding whether to take a break from studying is an option that should be considered. Some students stand by their choice to take some time off straight after finishing high school and use it to muster up some funds to travel overseas. Others recommend going straight into university and then using the extended breaks between semesters and each academic year to go sightseeing. Then, you have those who choose to take time off in between their courses. There is no 'best' option here. It really depends on whether you have a burning desire to travel after graduating from high school, are feeling burnt out and need a break from studying, or are keen to start studying post-school and travel when you have the time. I did a small amount of travelling between semesters and then decided to explore Europe for three months with my boyfriend once I had finished my postgraduate diploma of psychology. I hadn't travelled much with my family when I was younger, so the opportunity to see new countries, experience different cultures and expand my horizons was something that I had always wanted to do. These years are some of the most exciting you will experience as you begin to test what personal independence is really like! The important point to remember here is to take some time off from studying - whether it is to travel, work, or anything else — when it feels right. Only you will be able to tell when that is! One thing I will say is this; some of my most special moments and most cherished memories are from my time spent travelling overseas. Travelling is a different kind of learning and it can teach you many life lessons. You simply have to open yourself up to them.

My Top 5 Tips
For Deciding A Career Pathway

 Brainstorm a range of degrees and careers that spark your interest, before narrowing down your list.

 Speak to older students and people in your desired profession to find out more about a degree or career.

 Find out which universities are best known for the degrees you are interested in studying.

 Attend an open day at a university to find out more about the facilities and courses on offer.

 Consider taking time off from studying for travel or work.

My Final Words of Wisdom

As we come to the end of the book, I pass on to you these final words of wisdom in the hope that they will resonate with you throughout your academic journey: Know that you have the power to accomplish great things in life. Remind yourself of this when life brings you new challenges. Embrace them and rise up to them. Be open to learning new skills and expanding your horizons. That's what your time at school and university is for! It's your time to begin creating yourself and the life you want to live. What kind of life will you choose? How will you contribute to society? Keep this is mind as you continue on this exciting adventure. Remember that although your surroundings may change – that eventually you will leave behind your classroom, teachers and peers – your education doesn't stop there. We never stop learning. Each opportunity in life brings with it new and important skills, and while it may not be clear how each one may serve you in the future, eventually you will see that they all do.

Acknowledgements

To my teachers, each and every one of you has shared so many valuable lessons over the years. Your love for teaching and dedication to your students has truly inspired and instilled in me a love for learning.

To the team at Mango Media Inc. and my editor Hugo, you believed in this project from the very beginning and have helped to make my dream a reality. To my dearest friends, you have all been a part of my wonderful journey and helped shape my experience at school and university. Thank you for reassuring me in times of stress and teaching me the importance of finding a balance in life. To my future family in law, thank you for taking me under your wing and supporting all that I do. Each and every one of you has a special place in my heart.

To my wonderful big family++, you have all collectively shaped the person I am today. There is something incredibly special about growing up with a strong support system like I have. To my big sister Michelle, growing up, you have always been one to set an example. Thank you for your ongoing support and words of encouragement. I am grateful not only to call you my sister, but also my best friend. To my incredible parents, thank you for all of the sacrifices you have made for our family. You have taught me the value of hard work and I have you both to thank for my education. Thank you for always supporting, loving and believing in me, especially in my doubting moments. To my loving partner Adam, your unwavering support has empowered me and given me the courage to soar. Thank you for all of those reassuring long talks, for being so patient and for loving me unconditionally.

And most of all, to my viewers, your appreciation for your education and determination to succeed, is what drives me daily to continue on this exciting journey.

Author Bio

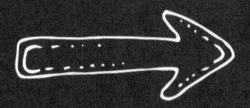

Jessica Holsman, AKA Study With Jess, is one of the growing stars on YouTube and the founder of seed.ED Educationery, the first ever educational designer stationery line for students. With millions of viewers flocking to her channel, Jess has established herself as the voice of students online. Offering up detailed and creative ways of studying, she connects with her audience on a personal level, which has allowed her to help students across the globe increase their grades, develop better social skills and enjoy high school. The young study tips guru and savvy entrepreneur has made it her mission to bring an element of fun into even the most mundane homework tasks!

Let's be friends

Follow me to stay in touch and keep
up to date with the latest news!

Study With Jess

youtube.com/studywithjess
facebook.com/studywithjess
@studywithjess
@studywithjess

Share your study inspiration posts
with me #studywithjess

seed.ED Educationery

facebook.com/seedededucationery
@seed.ed_educationery
@seededofficial

Share your seed.ED Educationery study
posts with me #seeded

CPSIA information can be obtained
at www.ICGtesting.com
Printed in the USA
BVOW11s1930300617
488191BV00002B/4/P